Peony — Lisa Rogney

Call Me Lisa

Lisa Rogney

Gayle Siebert

Published by Gayle Siebert, 2021.

While every precaution has been taken in the preparation of this book, the publisher assumes no responsibility for errors or omissions, or for damages resulting from the use of the information contained herein.

CALL ME LISA

First edition. May 24, 2021.

Copyright © 2021 Gayle Siebert.

ISBN: 978-1775347552

Written by Gayle Siebert.

Table of Contents

Pacific Chorus 1
Changes 9
Party Time 20
Nikki and Jackson 37
Back to School 44
Hurricane 60
Angie Meets Jarrett 68
Against the World 73
Dylan 83
Trent 88
Stormy Weather 96
She's back 105
Something Special 114
Frosty 119
Sehr Goot 130
Show Time 137
Nikki and Trevor 150
Real Life 156
Eighteen 162
Fall Guy 164
A Dish Served Lukewarm 173
AUTHOR'S NOTES 182

Pacific Chorus

CALL ME LISA. OKAY, I know you're going to say that's the opening line from Moby Dick but with my name substituted for Ishmael, and High Five to you. In my defense, I'm totally stumped for an idea. Mrs. Wiebe, my creative writing teacher, insists we write something, Period, No Excuses. Not even Severe Writer's Block cuts any ice with her. She's pretty, and she's usually nice too, but sometimes she climbs on her High Horse and acts like an Authority Figure and can even be just plain Bossy. Of course it's not just acting, because she's the teacher and I'm sure you know that means she has Authority Figure and Bossy built right in.

Anyway. Mrs. Wiebe claims that just by starting to write something you'll get tons of ideas and before you know it, you'll be inspired and will be going at it like there's no tomorrow. So far this morning that hasn't happened, even though I started off with a totally catchy first sentence which must have been plenty inspirational for Herman Melville because look where his story went from there! Maybe it's just that Ishmael is more inspirational than Lisa as names go, but I'm glad my name isn't Ishmael just the same.

If you're thinking I'll fail this class or there will be some other unhappy consequence if I don't get the assignment done, you can forget it. It's for a summer writing camp I'm taking at Vancouver Island University because I've decided to become an author. I've always done lots of reading, even old books no one ever bothers with, such as *American Captain* and *Peyton Place,* and you guessed it, *Moby Dick.* So you see, I'm a natural!

If you're wondering why I would read *Peyton Place*, it's because in one of our discussions in my Creative Writing Class, Mrs. Wiebe mentioned that in 1950-something it was so scandalous it was banned. Compared to *Fifty Shades of Gray* which wasn't banned or *Lady Chatterly's Lover* which was, it's a children's book. If you're interested in getting an idea of how things have changed since the Fifties, go ahead and read *Peyton Place* but if you're looking for something worth banning a book for, I recommend the other two.

Anyway, I've always loved words, especially big ones with lots of syllables, and I make a point of learning a new one every day. If you want to do this, all you have to do is find a word you don't know the meaning of, look it up, and then use it in a sentence as soon as possible. If you go online to Mirriam–Webster, you can sign up for their Word of the Day email. It's cool because it also explains what the word means. This is important! I can't stress this enough! If you use a word incorrectly you will not only look like an idiot but it won't count toward your New Word Every Day totals. You can keep track as I do on a little calendar, or come up with your own system like maybe a computer spreadsheet.

It goes without saying The New Word Every Day total is on the honour system. If you cheat, you're only cheating yourself. It does make for some strange looks, though, should you come out with a sentence like: "Polydactylism is quite common in cats and not as rare in humans as you might think" out of the blue. Sometimes even if you wait all day, there isn't a suitable lead-in even if you try and start a conversation by saying something like: "Did you know quite a few people are born with extra fingers and toes?" If no one says anything and you need it for your Word of The Day, you just have to go ahead and spit it out. So it's important to take care when choosing the word. Avoid words that haven't been used by anyone for decades, or that are too specific such as polydactylism.

Since being in this course I've discovered my writing skills aren't as top shelf as I thought. It came as a surprise after years of nothing but glowing parental reviews. Not that I'm completely without talent; if you asked Mrs. Wiebe, she'd probably say something like "Lisa shows promise" but you realize that's not much of a compliment and is more in the Damning With Faint Praise category. I might be discouraged if I didn't think she was wrong. Not a hundred percent wrong, but wrong at least to a degree. A large degree.

As I mentioned, Mrs. Wiebe is nice and would never discourage anyone which is not to say she isn't capable of finding fault. She is. For instance, she says I should never use a Big Word where a Little Word will do and I shouldn't capitalize things that aren't Proper Nouns and my sentences are too long and are sometimes put together with Comma Splices or an excessive number of 'ands' so they're often Run-On Sentences, and I should make two or even three sentences instead. And also never begin a sentence with "and". I've tried, but I get going and don't want to interrupt the flow which is what happens when you put in a period instead of a comma, periods being Full Stops after all, and besides, I like using capitals as it adds extra emphasis. I tell her I'm developing my own style. From her lukewarm response to that explanation it's obvious I'm going to have to come up with a more compelling argument or just become another sheep and go along with *The Industry Canada Style Guide for Writers and Editors* she had us download from the government website.

Short sentences or long, I'm usually able to come up with some ideas. It's the longest assignment she's given us, only fitting as it's the last one of the course, but still, it's only a fifteen-hundred-word story and I should be able to bash something out in a couple of hours. Yet here I sit, staring at the monitor, with no rush of plot ideas assaulting me. It may be harder than I thought for my writing career to take off and I'm going to need a Good Education to get that Real Job Dad is always mentioning. It's probably a little too soon to pass on the pre-matriculation courses when I sign up for my Grade Twelve subjects next week.

Maybe the reason I haven't come up with any ideas today is that I have a lot on my mind. Summer vacation is nearly over so there's back to school to worry about, I haven't heard from my boyfriend for a week despite sending him a couple of texts, and then there's Angie and what she's going through right now.

Angie has been my best friend since last winter. I know it's not nice to be jealous of your best friend, but I have been since the day I met her, for two reasons: one, she's gorgeous with nice creamy brown skin that never gets zits, not even in that little crease at the side of her nose; and two, although her parents are very strict her mother lets her use her car whenever she wants, which is most of the time, so it's almost like hers. She even has a credit card to pay for gas and she's allowed to use it for other things too. Anyone would be jealous of that, right? But I'm not real proud of myself for being jealous of her now because—

There's a crash outside my door like something fell against it and Big Mutt bursts into my room with my little brother, Jemmy, right behind him.

"Hey!" I say. Actually, it's more of a *yell* than a *say*, because Big Mutt stepped on my bare foot. If you have figured out from his name that he's a big dog, High Five to you. I love him but when he steps on your foot, which happens a lot because he's very klutzy, it hurts just the same. "Don't you know how to knock?"

"I did knock," Jemmy says. His hands are cupped together like he's got something trapped in there, which explains why his knock was more of a thump. A feeling of dread washes over me. I wish we had the kind of door knobs you have to turn which would mean he couldn't open the door with his hands clasped together like that, rather than the lever type which even Big Mutt and Bitsy can open. If you have a little brother, you understand.

"Well, for one, that wasn't a knock and for two, you're supposed to wait for someone to say come in!"

"Sorry," Jemmy says, "but look what I've got!" He opens his cupped hands to show me a little frog. I've seen them in the marsh at the end of our field.

"Oh yeah, a frog."

"He's a Pacific Chorus Frog. Isn't he cute? Can I use your aquarium? It's already got sand in it but I'll have to take most of it out and then I'll have to add some water but then it will be perfect and I can keep him in it!"

"Yes, he's cute, but you can't keep him because he'll die and anyway, you can't have my aquarium."

"No he won't die! I'll take care of him."

"He'll be lonesome without all his friends. And what are you going to feed him?"

"I'm going to go catch some friends for him. And I'll feed him, um, frog food."

"What if the other frogs you get aren't his friends? They could be frogs he doesn't like, did you think of that? Besides, you know it's wrong to keep him. You should just take a picture of him and put him back where you found him."

"I only want to watch him for a little while." His shoulders slump at my lack of enthusiasm. The frog squirms as though getting ready to leap and he closes his hands around it again. For a second, I feel sorry for taking the wind out of his sails. Only for a second, though.

"Anyway, can you see the sand is all layers of different colours?"

He shrugs his shoulders and says, "Yeah? So?"

"So it's, umm, decoration. Art."

"But you're not using it and I need it! Couldn't I have it? Please?"

I'm about to explain how *Art* doesn't have to be actively used, when I have a better look at Big Mutt. As usual he has his happy dog smiley face. His tongue is lolling out, he's wagging his tail and he's fixated on

Jemmy's hands. I begin to wonder if he played a role in catching the frog. I'm just now noticing how wet and dirty he is.

"Oh my gawd, you're filthy! Get out of here, dog!" I get to my feet and point to the door. There's already a trail of dirty paw prints in the carpet. Was there no parent to run interference before these two got to my room?

The dog looks at me as if he suddenly doesn't understand what *out* means. My cat, Bitsy, who's been curled up on my pillow since I got up, looks at me with one gimlet eye as if to say, if you insist on letting that dog in the house, what do you expect? (Forgive me but I've been dying to use that *gimlet eye* phrase.)

"I'm going to ask Mom," Jemmy says. He turns and scurries out the door ahead of Big Mutt.

"She won't make me give you my aquarium!" I call after him.

Then I start to feel bad, because I'm tired of the dumb-looking thing anyway. If you think I bought all that coloured sand for nothing because it didn't turn out nearly as well as I had pictured it, High Five to you. Those things look better in fancy jars I guess. It could also be that to keep costs down I used dirt for some of the layers. I thought it would be a nice counterpoint. It isn't. It just looks like dirt. Once it's in, it's pretty well impossible to get out.

Because of the Aquarium Sand Feature and other projects with surprisingly poor outcomes, I've decided I no longer want to be an artist or a sculptor and then of course there's the author thing I mentioned so I don't need the aquarium for an art portfolio and anyway, it's too ugly to put in a portfolio if I had one, which I don't. I guess I should go and tell him he can have it after all.

As brothers go, he's a good one I guess. Other boys his age are into riding bikes, quads, or even motorbikes rather than wading around mucky water in search of swamp creatures. For example, his used-to-be best friend, Devon. Devon lives across the road. He and Jemmy once spent hours together, much of it out in the marsh, and now Devon spends most of his time with Trent, the older boy who moved in down the road this summer, because Trent has a little dirt bike and lets him ride it.

Everything I know about Trent I learned from Jemmy, because he goes with Devon to Trent's sometimes. The bike Trent lets Jemmy and Devon use was his until he outgrew it, and Trent and his dad have built trails through the bush. Part of the trail is next to the road but not right on it, so you can ride all around their property and never have to go where there might be traffic. Sounds like fun, and safe, too, right?

But Jemmy is only mildly interested in riding on or tinkering with things motorized and would rather poke around the muck in the ditches or go to the marsh, even without Devon. I don't know who Jemmy's best friend is now. Maybe he doesn't have one. I know what that feels like; I lost my friends last year because they got other interests, too.

In Jemmy's favour he spends hours on his tablet researching everything he finds. He's got piles of Grammy's old Book-Of-The-Month Club books with different kinds of swamp plants pressed between the pages, and boxes with dead fauna: shrews, mice, voles and so on that Bitsy killed but didn't eat, or birds that died of natural causes if you call flying into the living room window a natural cause. But his first love is the slithery creepy crawly hoppy things he keeps in pill dispensers and empty margarine containers. So far he hasn't kept any live specimens. At least not to my knowledge.

He's on an endless quest to find one of the brightly-coloured lizards or snakes he keeps showing me on his tablet and isn't deterred by the fact they aren't indigenous even though that means it is never going to happen. I'm kind of proud of him for that, for the research I mean, even though at times he yammers on about all he's learned long after I've heard all I need to know, just because he likes sharing facts.

If you think the best part of him being a budding naturalist is that we don't have the noise of motors around here all the time and that he's quiet when he's on his tablet doing his research or skulking around the marsh hunting for more slithery creepy crawly hoppy things, High Five to you! Still, it's kind of funny that last year I would've given anything for him to quit making stupid noises constantly and now I kind of miss it. Didn't see that coming.

Hmm. Slithery things. The marsh. The inspiration for my Creative Writing Assignment has just presented itself.

Changes

WE LIVE ON AN ACREAGE on the outskirts of town. We moved here shortly after Jemmy was born. I'm not sure why we moved here, because neither Mom nor Dad has the slightest interest in keeping horses or any other animals except for, you know, Big Mutt and Bitsy. (Big and Bitsy. Get it?)

Dad grumbles about how much work it is. Mom always tells him he doesn't need to mow the lawn twice a week and we could fence it off so more is in the pasture and less is lawn, or he could quit fertilizing and turn off the irrigation to the half behind the house so it doesn't grow so fast. He always acted as if those were dumb ideas until the day he announced he was going to turn the irrigation to the back section of lawn off, like he just thought of it so now it's a good idea. Mom snorted (I see where I get it from) and threw up her hands.

I guess it was Mom who wanted to live here in the first place, and she talked Dad into it. At least twice a week she makes a comment about how peaceful it is not having traffic whizzing by and neighbours looking over the fence. If Dad is within hearing distance he can be counted on to say neither of those things bothers him and then he will start in about the large lawn.

I think Dad likes mowing the lawn. I know for sure he likes riding around on his BNM (Big New Mower) if not actually mowing, possibly because it has a drink holder. If he lets it go past the three-and-a-half days mark, mowing the lawn can be a Three Beer Job. I'm not sure what he'll do in the winter although he has been mentioning there is a snow scraper attachment available. He might be able to use that once or twice a year. I don't think he'd want to be drinking beer if it was cold enough to snow, though, so I don't know if he's thought it through.

I love living out in the country! I admit it has its downside even though I don't have to mow the lawn which I wouldn't want to do for two reasons: one, it wastes time I could be doing things I'm more interested in such as advancing my writing career; and two, I don't like beer.

If you're wondering about the downside I mentioned, there are two so really, so I should have said down*sides*: one, since I don't drive (yet) I miss out on doing after school things; and two, it takes about an hour to walk home if I miss the school bus. There is a city bus but it only runs out this far a couple of times a day and usually not when you would want to go anywhere.

I mostly don't mind walking home. I don't have to walk on the road because there's a paved trail most of the way so it's easy going, but it's no fun in the dark especially in the forested part. In winter, when it gets dark at like four o'clock, I make sure I don't miss the school bus.

You're probably thinking since I'm old enough to drive, maybe I should save my McDonald's wages and buy a car or maybe if my parents can afford this big house they should give me one, but I don't have my license yet anyway so it's not a priority or front of mind as they say now. Besides, I'm saving up for a saddle and I want to get that before I get a car.

I'm working on getting my driver's license too, but Mom doesn't have much time to take me practice driving since she's started going to Pilates classes or self-improvement night courses at VIU or her remedial pottery group, one or the other of which seems to be going on every night. Since her promotion, her job sometimes takes her away from home too. So she doesn't have a lot of spare time.

And Dad, as I mentioned, prefers to drive around the lawn on his BNM or hang out in the shed polishing his BNM. Full disclosure?

He would take me driving, but after a couple of tries, I don't ask him anymore. After a driving lesson with him, I would start drinking beer, whether I like it or not.

Or maybe you're thinking I'm old enough and I can tell time so I should be better organized and not miss the bus. I've already admitted being capable of it in the winter. You're right, it's a poor argument for me to make and I ought to withdraw it, so there really is only one downside.

Anyway. There are plenty of upsides to living here, such as the school bus thing. It is a built-in excuse not to go out for after-school activities such as basketball because it would make me miss the bus.

The PE teacher is always bugging me to try out for basketball. I'm one of the tallest girls in school so she's positive I must like basketball, but I Plus Plus **DO NOT!** All that running around getting sweaty just to catch a ball you're not supposed to hang onto anyway. Softball I understand, and it's in the spring when the days are longer so it's no big deal walking home after.

The main upside to living here is Peony. If you figured out from the pasture and saddle comments that there must be a horse, High Five to you! Peony, my horse, lives in the barn at the back of our property and has a stall she can go into or not, her choice, plus the field next to all that lawn I mentioned.

I got Peony a little while after Wembly died. I thought getting another horse would dishonor Wembly's memory but the more I thought about it, the more I came around to the idea it's the opposite. Like, Wembly was such a good boy and I loved him so much, I wanted another relationship like that. So, in the spring, I got Peony from the horse and donkey rescue I volunteer at.

Peony is a lot bigger than Wembly was. In fact, she's big compared to most horses, seventeen-two if you know what that is. (If you do, skip the rest of this paragraph. If you don't, and you really want to know, read on.) She is seventeen hands two inches high at her withers.

Withers is where her neck joins her back and a horse's height is always measured there. In Canada and a lot of other countries, the height is given in hands, and a hand is four inches.

I've mentioned Peony is seventeen two or seventeen hands two inches, so she's seventy inches, or a hundred and seventy-eight centimeters if you're German or have some other reason for not knowing what inches are, or five foot ten inches tall if that gives you a better idea. If you put a ruler across from her withers to the top of my head, it would be level.

Anyway. She is a big horse not just in height but all over because she's a draft cross, one of her parents being a work horse. Although she's really big, she's super gentle and already loves me even when I'm not bringing her food. Maddy, the lady who runs the rescue, bought her out of a kill pen so she wouldn't be sent to slaughter. Thinking about horses being killed makes me sad and when you think it could have been Peony, just ten years old and so sweet and with so much life ahead of her, it's enough to make a person cry. It's even worse when it's the really young ones who are sentenced to death just because nobody bought them. I try not to dwell on it and you shouldn't either but keep it in mind in case you ever have a chance to speak out against it.

The importance of speaking out against things that are wrong is one of the things I've been thinking about lately. Maybe it's because of what I see at the rescue. Maybe it's what Dad calls Growing Up and Mom calls getting a Social Conscience, but I've been thinking about a lot of things differently. For example, I am now mostly vegan or what Dad calls being a Fussy Eater, although I haven't given up tuna yet.

Mom is mostly vegan too although she still eats cheese as do I so on pizza nights, we share a vegetarian. But me eating tuna and Mom and me eating cheese isn't enough to get either of us off Dad's Fussy Eater list.

A while ago, Mom quit cooking meat because she hates smelling or touching it, so if Dad wants it he has to cook it. He grumbles, but I don't think he really minds because he's got this huge barbeque in the covered area right outside the kitchen door and you can find him out there polishing it when he's not polishing the BNM.

You might be wondering why he needs such a huge barbeque to cook one steak or a couple of wieners. Well, friends or clients of Dad's who have boats and like to fish occasionally give him a big salmon and he needs the big barbeque then. Mom and I eat salmon then too, because it was humanely caught and also, it would be very wrong to waste it.

If Dad is resigned to Mom not cooking meat, it doesn't stop him from being cranky about her not buying it for him. She says it makes her sick to even look at all that meat. She doesn't like going into the meat section of the grocery store because she can't stop thinking about all the terrified animals that were killed for those packages of flesh. At this point in the discussion Dad always says she's as unreasonable about Those Who Eat Meat As Humans Were Meant To, as Reformed Smokers are about People Who Smoke. Everyone knows they are the worst. She points out that he knows where the store is as well as she does, and wonders why it is her job to buy the groceries anyway. In case he hasn't noticed, she works too. So if he wants meat, he not only has to cook it, but buy it too. Mom does sometimes make bacon on week-ends, but I have a feeling it's not as much for Dad as for Jemmy because Jemmy loves bacon almost as much as frogs.

Just to clarify in case you're wondering, Jemmy doesn't eat frogs, that's not what I meant. The frogs he catches are too small in any case but even if he caught one of the big bullfrogs that's an introduced species taking over all the wetlands and is the type they use for frog's legs, I don't think he'd eat it. Not because he wants to be vegan. He just loves frogs too much.

You might be wondering about the bullfrogs and who would think of bringing them here. Someone had an idea for a frog legs farm and imported a bunch of bullfrogs from Louisiana or Alabama or someplace where they actually eat them. When the business flopped they just let them all go and now we have these giant bullfrogs on Vancouver Island, eating the little frogs that have been here for thousands of years. Bullfrogs can eat anything that fits in their mouth which includes ducklings and I'm sure you agree that isn't pleasant either for the duckling or the mommy duck who might be watching.

You should never catch tadpoles but if you do, remember to put them back where you got them and never let them go in another pond in case they turn out to be bullfrogs. We don't want to spread them around, because we want our own frogs to survive and our frogs are just a tasty little snack for a bullfrog so they can eat lots of them and before long the whole marsh would have nothing but bullfrogs which you can imagine wouldn't make the ducks happy.

You have Jemmy to thank for this information, but keep in mind it proves I pay attention to what he's nattering about at least some of the time.

Anyway. Back to Peony. That was her name when I got her although I think it was someone at the rescue who named her that because a lot of the horses and donkeys that came into the rescue last spring were given flower names like Petunia and Violet and Rose and Daisy. It wasn't so good for the boys, but I don't think they minded because we gave them weed names like Yarrow and Dandy Lion. Both of those have flowers too so they're still in the Flower Name category.

When we used up all the flower names we could think of, we started naming them after famous writers like Clancy and Crichton and McMurtry and Nelson and McKay and so on, which wasn't so great for the girls, so it evens out. If you think this was my suggestion because I'm going to be a writer so I've read books by those authors, High Five to you!

You have to name them something, because the ones that come from the auction just have a number stuck on their rumps and calling a living thing by a number could make you think they're not important like what happened to the Jews at Auschwitz and of course every life is important, even horses and donkeys and dogs and cats no one wants.

Peony is an okay name, except when I try to shorten it for a pet name, like PeePee. I don't have to explain why that isn't good, no matter how funny Jemmy thinks it is. He always calls her that and it cracks him up every time.

I'm not a ten-year-old boy, so I go with PeeNee or usually, NeeNee. She doesn't care what I call her. She acts like I'm the Sun and the Moon no matter what.

There is one thing wrong with NeeNee: she has just one eye. She wasn't born that way. Something bad happened to her. You wouldn't believe the nice things my Facebook friends commented when I posted her story and everyone said she's beautiful even missing an eye. Whatever happened to her is another thing to be sad about, but you have to keep in mind she has a good life now and I will never, ever let anyone hurt her and she'll never be in a kill pen again.

Because of her missing eye, you have to be careful about coming up to her on that side and make sure you call out like you would when approaching any horse from behind, so she knows you're there. If you don't, she can get startled and spook. This can also happen when you're riding her, if she turns her head and sees something, like a person, standing there that she didn't know about. Once it was a big leaf falling off the maple tree at the side of the road.

At least when she spooks, it's just a jump and a little scoot and she never does anything bad like bucking or running away. Still, it's always fast and unexpected and makes my heart pound for a second or two. She doesn't spook because she's stupid or mean or wants me to fall off because she would never do anything to hurt me; it's just that horses are a prey species, so they always have to be vigilant.

This being Saturday, I have a riding lesson before my afternoon shift at McDonald's. I'm on NeeNee in my old western saddle walking briskly along the path next to the pavement, on my way to the big horse farm where my coach, Elke, lives. Elke is super nice! Her lessons are great, too. She isn't the kind of coach who yells at you although she does make you do stuff you might prefer not to, such as staying right next to the rail when you go past the place where NeeNee thinks a Gremlin lives, not just once but again and again and again. And again.

In NeeNee's defense, there is a bush there and anyone would agree it looks like a good Gremlin Hiding Place. On top of that, Elke's Jack Russell, Dixie, often lies in the shade there. Although Dixie doesn't do anything horrible such as jumping out and nipping at Peony's heels, when Peony is on Gremlin Watch, Dixie suddenly racing off after someone coming up the driveway is bad enough. Since Elke has a German accent I can always act like I didn't quite get what she was saying and let NeeNee move off the rail a safe distance.

If you ever need to know what a safe-from-Gremlin-attack distance is, I recommend going with NeeNee's estimate of about a meter.

Of course if it's on her blind side, she doesn't care at all and stays right on the rail. On those occasions I smile and give Elke a triumphant look like there's nothing to it and the times we're off the track are purely accidental.

You're probably thinking I must be a poor student if I'm constantly playing dumb, but you can forget about it! I like Elke, I want her to like me, I really want to be a good dressage rider and I love getting lessons, so I try hard and reserve my dumb act for things I really don't want to do, like tapping NeeNee on her flank again when she kicked out the first time I tapped her with the whip, even though I'm a hundred per cent sure she won't buck. Maybe only ninety-eight per cent, because she has done a Feel-Good Buck a couple of times.

When Peony does something like spooking or giving a little buck, Elke always says, "Didn't happen". This seems an odd thing to say because in fact it did happen and I know she saw it because she doesn't miss a thing, even things you wish she did, such as being too far off the rail at the Gremlin Bush.

Elke's farm is at the end of our road, next to the Christmas tree farm. There isn't much traffic since it's a dead-end, but you do have to go past Trent's house and you never know when he might come racing out along the trail next to the road on a dirt bike or quad. NeeNee doesn't seem to care, though, maybe because you can always hear him coming.

Trent looks cool, if a little lumpy, when he wears the clothes that protect his various body parts should he hit the dirt. I am careful not to gawk, though, for two reasons: one, he's hot, with wide shoulders, narrow hips and muscular legs and so he probably has lots of girls after him; and two, that would not be cool and besides, I have a boyfriend or at least I think I do. Maybe that's three things. Today, it's all quiet by the road, although I can hear something buzzing around in the bush at the back of his property. I won't lie. I'm a little disappointed.

I should add more in respect to Trent. Like I mentioned, he moved into our neighbourhood at the beginning of summer vacation and although Jemmy has been to his place, I haven't met him yet. I'm guessing he's good looking, because I've only seen him a few times and only when he's on his dirt bike wearing his full-face helmet. You have to give him credit for being safety-conscious but if you think it's a little disappointing that he's never stopped to say hey, High Five to you. He may be afraid of horses. A lot of people are and you can't blame them because they are big animals and NeeNee is bigger than most.

You might be wondering why I even care whether Trent is good looking or not. I don't, really, for two reasons: one, what a person looks like is not important; and two: as I mentioned, I have a boyfriend. His name is Dwayne Johnson. (Not *that* Dwayne Johnson!) I met Dwayne at the rescue last spring. He was a volunteer too, so besides being taller than me and very hot, he's also an Animal Lover which is a Big Plus in any human but especially a boyfriend. Until the end of the school year we were together nearly every day. I haven't seen much of him since he left to go to work on a ranch in Alberta, though. In fact, the only time I've seen him since he left is when we Skype or Facetime.

I'm starting to think Dwayne won't be coming back. He's older than I am, finished Grade Twelve, and although he talked about going to Vancouver Island University right here in Nanaimo, lately he's been mentioning he might take a year off. You know, have a break from studying, give his brain a rest, make some money for tuition and so on. He hasn't said so, but I worry he plans to do that in Alberta.

Also, it seems like we Skype less often than we did at first, and he seems a bit distracted or not as warm or friendly in the way of making Suggestive Comments like he used to be. Maybe it's my imagination but our sessions seem shorter, too. He signs off by saying something like, "Well I'm bushed. I'm gonna hit the hay," and so on. I guess they work him really hard on that ranch and also I have to keep in mind it's an hour later in Alberta so he's not really going to bed at eight o'clock.

Anyway. Peony and I arrive at Elke's, go through the yard past the indoor ring to the outdoor ring, and I get off. Elke is already there, teaching Marci. Marci is old, maybe as old as Mom because her daughter, Bailey, is only a little older than me and will be going to Vancouver Island University when school starts. Bailey has a horse and takes lessons from Elke, too. Marci and Bailey are both way, way more advanced dressage riders than I am, which is to be expected since they've been at it a lot longer. Also, they keep their horses at Elke's and since there's that indoor ring I mentioned, they can ride year round, rain or shine.

I've had a horse since I was nine so nearly half my life, but all I did up until now was plunk around the neighbourhood and then mostly just in good weather. Also I don't have that dressage saddle I mentioned I'm saving up for. You might think I'm hampered by that, but right now I'm just learning basics such as how to tell Peony which lead I want her to take, keeping her straight, teaching her to stay in whatever gait I ask her for in a nice consistent rhythm, which diagonal I should rise on at trot, and so on. You know, stuff I never knew about, thought about or cared about before. Luckily that stuff is the same whether you ride English or Western so I should be okay when I finally do get my dressage saddle.

You're probably wondering why I still need lessons when I've been riding for so long. People ask me that all the time. If that's what you're thinking, just remember it's complicated. Think about it: you know how to walk, but you have to learn how to dance. Peony is ten years old but she's a beginner at this just like I am so we're learning together. Elke says it would be easier for me on a horse that already knows what she's supposed to do but Peony is the horse I have and I wouldn't trade her for a trained dressage horse even if I could. It's not ideal because Elke has to teach both of us.

Elke spots me at the gate and waves me in, so I lead NeeNee through the gate and over to the mounting block to get back on. All I have to do while I'm waiting for Marci's lesson to end is to go around the ring staying out of the way. That's not as easy as you might think since they're starting in on flying changes across the diagonal which means cantering from the corner on one side of the ring to the far corner on the other side, changing leads every few strides, then around the short end of the ring and across the diagonal the other way and sometimes she just makes a circle or doesn't go the full length, so I never know which direction I should be going to stay out of the way.

I quit thinking about Dwayne or Trent or Angie and start visualizing Peony and me doing flying changes. I can't even get Peony to take her left lead half the time, and Elke says we won't be doing flying lead changes until we have mastered simple changes which means left lead canter, trot, right lead canter and even left lead canter, walk, and right lead canter. See? I told you it was complicated!

If you think changes are awfully far in the future for Peony and me, High Five to you. Luckily we are both young so we've got time. Also, I'm determined, or as Dad would tell you, Stubborn.

Party Time

MOM IS GOING INTO TOWN so she lets me drive to work. We make it with a minute to spare and without incident, if you don't count when I cut that pedestrian off for that last right turn. He had barely taken a step off the curb so technically he should have waited for me to go by, in my opinion, and besides, if I waited for every pedestrian to dawdle across the crosswalk we wouldn't have gotten here on time.

Mom didn't see it quite that way and said she doesn't care if I'm late, there is no excuse for terrifying a pedestrian; I should have come home from Elke's sooner so we could have left earlier, and so on. I have explained many times that there is a Time Warp Containment Field at Elke's. I don't think it's only at Elke's, but it's especially strong there. Mom is a hard sell on that one.

Anyway. Since she's still a little cranky about the pedestrian thing I don't linger; I stop near the door and get out, grabbing my backpack out of the back seat. Mom gets out and comes around to get into the driver's seat.

"Thanks, Mom," I say, and give her a big smile so she knows I'm not holding her bad attitude against her. "Don't forget the Cinnaswirl! Maybe get two this time!"

For the uninitiated, Cinnaswirl is stuff you add to coffee to make it drinkable. I started putting it in my coffee last spring, which is when I started drinking coffee. Mom likes it too, so we go through a lot of it. She's still not smiling as she drives off. I guess I shouldn't have reminded her about the Cinnaswirl because the day started off with her a having a little cranky fit when she came down for coffee and found I used almost all of it. Of course I left some for her, but apparently not enough. The bottle is opaque so how was I to know how much was still in there? And another point in my defense: she drinks her coffee black as often as she adds Cinnaswirl and there is no way of knowing which way she is going to want it on a particular day.

But this morning you'd think her whole day was going to be ruined because she didn't get enough Cinnaswirl. She went on about how it was almost half full yesterday and I might just as well warm up the Cinnaswirl and forget the coffee. I know she doesn't mean it, especially now that's she's so health conscious and Cinnaswirl not being what anyone would consider a Healthy Drink, warmed up or not. It's just her way of suggesting I use too much.

Anyway. I head for the door and pull it open, stopping inside for a second as a shudder at the screams and shrieks of the Monster Children courses through my body. I wonder why they didn't put an Employee Only door on the outside. I take a deep breath and soldier on. I make it safely through throngs of customers to the employee break room, where I put my things away and get ready to hustle out to the drive-through window.

Jimmy comes in about two seconds after me. He's just finishing his shift and I'm due to start about five minutes ago so we don't have time to yak.

"Hey," he says, "how was your lesson?"

"Pretty good," I tell him. "Got left lead a few times and once, Elke said 'there's your trot.'"

"But you trot all the time. What does that mean, 'there's your trot'?"

"Something about not just leg moving. The flow of energy over the back. It's complicated." I throw in a theatrical sigh as if it's really difficult and Peony and I must be making serious progress if Elke saw where my trot was. I'm afraid he's going to ask for more details. He's such a detail guy it can be annoying at times. Since I don't have a hot clue and can't begin to explain it, I hurry on before he can ask me to.

"Hey, you talk to Angie about coming tonight?"

"Yeah. She says she's staying in."

This isn't good. Angie has been staying home so much I've hardly seen her all summer. It's puzzling, because for months we hung out every day and now she'd rather stay home? She says she's tired or she doesn't feel like doing anything. Lots of times she just doesn't answer my texts or phone calls at all and tells me her phone was upstairs being charged or she couldn't find it.

Mom noticed the Lack of Angie and when I complained about all these things to her, she said it sounds like Angie's depressed and who can blame her?

"I'll call her later. And don't worry, I'll get Mom to drive with me and pick you up if she doesn't change her mind."

"It's okay. I'll ride my bike!" He makes a double thumbs up and shows every tooth in his head. It's always a surprise to me that he has such a nice smile, having had no dental care up until a couple of months ago.

You might wonder what there is about riding a bike instead of getting picked up that makes him so stoked he would give even one thumb up. It's because he's so in love with his bike. He bought it with one of his first pay cheques. He got it at the bike shop but it was a trade-in so it's not new, and it's not a fancy hundred and ninety-seven speed or anything, it's just he's never had a bike before. He's proud of it and takes good care of it. Would you believe, he takes it with him right into his hotel room even though he could much more easily lock it to a pole in the parking lot? That's how much he loves it.

Think about learning to ride a bike when you're fifteen! I shudder to imagine all the crashes that must have occurred before he was competent enough to head out into traffic. It's hard enough to learn when you're a little kid and Jimmy is not what you'd call well-coordinated.

A manager, the enormous one with the greasy hair I call Big Manager for obvious reasons but also because he's the boss of all the managers, comes thumpity-thumping into the break room and I try to shrink into the woodwork. Not easy when you're my size and there is no woodwork to be found. I wish Old Manager was on today, because she's a lot more reasonable in her expectations.

Anyway. Big Manager shows Jimmy his teeth, then sees me and the teeth disappear. From the look on his face, either his hemorrhoids have flared up or he's annoyed with me. Since I am now officially late and he's making stabbing motions at the wall clock with his pointing finger, I'm going with the latter, although it could be both I suppose.

I give him a winning smile and say to Jimmy, "See you later."

Being on the drive-through is kind of neat but stressful at the same time. It's not like being on the burger station. You have to do a lot of things besides just talking to customers through your headset and at the order window, and it's busy so you're going all the time. It does give me an excuse to talk to hot guys without seeming too interested in them, but they're very few and far between. Most of the customers are old people with kids.

Anyway. Four hours goes by pretty fast and I'm so busy I almost miss a cute guy. I do notice his car, though: red, with a spoiler and blacked-out windows. I think it might be Trent's because I've seen one just like it go by our place a lot. But then, there must be about a million red cars with spoilers so you can't go by that.

Today I notice a sticker of a dirt bike on the side window.

I pay more attention now and as he drives away I see there's a Monty's Motorcycle bumper sticker. That pretty well seals the deal; it was Trent and I wish I'd taken more than just a quick glance because now I can't even remember what colour his hair was. Blonde? Brown? He had a chance to say something to me when I handed him his order and his change, and we didn't make eye contact so I have to conclude he came because he was hungry and not because he was overcome with desire to meet me. Of course, he wouldn't know where I work. I feel better reminding myself of that.

It isn't until I think about it later I realize I missed a chance to invite him to the bonfire at our place tonight! But then, you can't go around inviting random guys to a party or they would think they're so special all they have to do is say one word and you'll be All Theirs, so I would have had to find out if it really was him first and how do you do that? Ask a guy who drives up to the take-out window, "Hey, are you Trent?" Dumb, right? So it wasn't really an Opportunity Missed, but more of an Embarrassing Moment Avoided.

When my shift is over, I text Angie from the break room. She might as well come to my place now and help getting things ready for the party and while she's at it, save me a walk home. I eat a Super-Size order of French fries while I wait for her to answer. I even send a follow-up smiley emoji. Still, she hasn't responded by the time I finish my fries, so I set out on foot.

I mentioned it takes about an hour to walk home from school. It's only a few minutes longer from McDonald's and most of it is along the Parkway. It's a paved path, no motor vehicles allowed, but you do have to watch out for bicycles and Intense Jogger-Mothers pushing strollers.

It's a nice afternoon and quite a pleasant walk except in the dark as I mentioned, especially where the path goes through the forested section, despite the smell of skunk cabbage from the swampy area. There's one spot where it's a bit above the highway and there's a great view of a lake, mountains, trees, hundreds of cars on the freeway, and so on. I'm not gawking around at scenery, though; I'm busy wondering if Mrs. Wiebe might have been blown away at the quality of my story since I was vigilant about comma splices, and now and then I worry about Angie.

I come to the spot where I have to cross the freeway. The light changes and I trot across. I continue jogging and I'm past the first turnoff when the red car with the spoiler and bumper stickers goes by and slows. I think it might pull over. I get a funny little thump of excitement in my chest and stop running. But my excitement is short lived as the car never completely stops and in a heartbeat it's off at regular speed again.

There were two people in the car, and the one in the passenger seat had long turquoise hair. If that was Trent's car, it looks like he has a girlfriend. For some reason I get a sinking feeling in the pit of my stomach. Then I remind myself I don't know where his family lived before, maybe nearby, so he could have a girlfriend right here in town and not have to bother getting a new one.

Also, you're my witness, I knew a lot of girls would be after him and I don't want to be one of a crowd, plus, you know, Dwayne, even though I don't know if we're still considered to be going steady.

The worst part is: the girl kind of looked like Nicole.

Nicole also lives on our road. She used to be my best friend and we spent a lot of time together back when she still had her pony. We rode all over the neighbourhood together, sat together on the school bus, walked home together, you know, we were BFFs. Then she sold her pony and last fall and started hanging with the popular kids in school. Before I knew it, she wasn't my friend anymore. On the rare occasions she didn't get a ride and had to take the bus, she walked right past without even looking at me and wouldn't sit next to me even if it was the last empty seat, which never happens but you get my point. Somehow I had become an Untouchable.

I should explain Untouchables in case you think I'm talking about Elliott Ness and the agents who captured Al Capone. I'm not. I'm talking about the Caste System in India. The lowest people in the system are the Dalit. I prefer the old term, Untouchables. If you're anywhere above them, especially if you are a Brahmin, you do not want to touch them although they are good enough to work for you, and you can tell them how much you're going to pay them or even find fault with what they did so at the end of the day you don't have to pay them at all. You don't have to concern yourself that they might have been relying on that day's wages to buy food for their family and now won't have anything to eat. If you have read *A Fine Balance*, you already know this.

I'm sure you agree the Caste System is wrong, but you shouldn't dwell on it. It is just another thing to keep in mind and speak out against if you get a chance.

Anyway. I'm not really an Untouchable for two reasons: one, we don't have a caste system (well, at least not one we admit to); and two: Nicole has never wanted me to work for her. I have no idea what kind of work she might want me to do and I wouldn't work for her if she lost her mind and asked me to anyway. Still, not having her as a friend makes me a little sad even now.

About the time Nicole stopped being my friend, I lost Jarrett as a friend, too. But that's a whole 'nother story.

On the plus side, I now have two new friends I might not have made otherwise: Jimmy and Angie. Besides them, Bailey from Elke's and some of the kids who volunteer at the rescue are also coming to the bonfire tonight. It's the second-last week-end before school starts again, so we're going to celebrate. There will be hot dogs of the regular chicken beaks and pig lips variety as well as vegan ones, pop, potato chips and so on. I have a lot to do to get ready, so I adjust my backpack and start jogging again.

BAILEY BROUGHT HER boyfriend, Andrew Cooper. "Call me Coop," he says to everyone as she introduces him. He's not very tall for a guy, not as tall as me, but he's Movie Star Handsome with dark hair long on top and just wavy enough so when it falls across his forehead it's in a kind of swirl, and intense brown eyes. I know from what Bailey has told me that his family is super rich, something related to the acres of greenhouses down in Cedar and they even have some in California.

Bailey's family is High Tone too and Dad is fond of saying Money Goes Where Money Is so probably the families have encouraged their relationship, plus Bailey isn't very tall so they're a good fit size-wise as couples go.

Alain (he's French Canadian) from the rescue brought his girlfriend Samantha and a couple of other kids who also work at the rescue, so with Jimmy and me and the other solos, there is a respectable number of people especially when you remember a year ago my only friends were Nicole and Jarrett.

Dad turned on the outdoor speakers and I got Coop to plug in his iPhone so we aren't listening to Old Fogie Music. It's a beautiful evening with not too many mosquitoes and everyone's chatting and laughing and once in a while people dance. I would say it's a great party. The only bad thing: Angie hasn't shown up yet.

There's a couple of things going on Mom wouldn't approve of: pot smoking and vaping. I see her come to the patio doors a couple of times and I know she realizes it's going on, but she must have decided to ignore it, both things being legal after all.

Besides those two things Mom wouldn't approve of, Coop is topping up people's Cokes with rum. He is old enough to drink legally, Coke does improve the taste of the rum, and it could account for a lot of the laughing. Coop came with Bailey in her car, and Alain/Samantha are the only other people who didn't get dropped off by someone, so as long as Bailey and one or the other of Alain/Samantha don't drink or smoke too much, it's okay. Besides, what can I do about it?

If you think this is the first time I ever drank booze, though, you can forget it. Nicole and I were frequent raiders of Dad's liquor cabinet since we were about twelve. Once, we drank so much rye, straight out of the bottle despite how awful it tasted, I had to add water so Dad wouldn't notice. He did notice, though, and when he did, yelled at me for about ten minutes. Mom didn't stick up for me, either. She joined in, saying things like *you have a fine brain* and *you have a mind of your own* and *you should know better than to go along with Nicole when she has bad ideas* and so on.

    I didn't think it was really all that bad as it didn't hurt anyone except ourselves, and there's got to be a first hangover for everyone so it makes sense to get it over with sooner rather than later, in my opinion. Neither of them saw it that way, though. I think the real reason Mom was choked was that she felt sorry for me, thinking I had the flu, so I got out of my Saturday chore of cleaning the Back Door Bathroom, which only has a sink and a toilet so it's not much of a job now that I look back on it but which I always whined about back then.

    Anyway, I realized that next time I would have to either add something to the rye to improve the colour in case it looked too pale watered down and that's what tipped Dad off, or go with vodka or gin instead. I never had to work it out because for the next few years, I couldn't find the key to the liquor cabinet. They must have decided it's okay for me to drink now because the key is back in its usual place. That's implied permission, right?

    As for pot, I've tried that too. I imagine everyone has. I didn't find it at all pleasant although possibly that's because I don't like smoking even regular tobacco. Also, at first it didn't affect me at all and then all of a sudden there was a buzzing noise behind my head and I thought bees were after me which anyone can understand spoils the experience.

    Anyway. When I talked to Angie just a couple of hours ago she promised she was coming but it's nearly nine, we've been roasting wieners and drinking rum and Coke for an hour, it's starting to get dark, and still no Angie. I text her: "whats ur ETA?" but no answer. If she doesn't get here soon, Coop may run out of rum!

    Just as I have that thought, I see her car pull into the driveway and come up to stop beside the garage. I hurry over and give her a quick hug as soon as she's clear of the door. "Are you okay?" I ask.

    Angie says, "Yeah. My aunt came and says she's staying the night and I should go have fun. Mom insisted, too." She takes a step away from me, and for a moment we listen to the sounds of the party on the patio just around the corner as she looks off across Peony's field. Then she mumbles, "I still feel guilty."

"Oh, Angie!" I say. I'm at a loss for words. Finally, I come up with: "Do you want to come and join the others or should we go to my room and just talk?"

"No, we can't do that! It's your...You're the host!" She sniffs. "I'll be lousy company. I should just go home."

"But you just got here! At least come and say hi to everyone!"

She looks dejected. I get it. She has plenty of reason to feel bad. When I think about it, I find my eyes filling and I catch my lower lip in my teeth, just to stop it from quivering. I notice Mom hovering around the front porch and she starts toward us.

"Hey, Angie!" she calls out.

"Hi, Mrs. Rogney," Angie responds.

Mom just waltzes up and grabs Angie and pulls her into a hug. To my astonishment, Angie starts crying. I would too if I didn't have such a good grip on my lip. It's just a natural reaction to seeing someone else crying.

Mom is saying things like it's okay, let it out, everything will be okay and so on even knowing everything will not be okay. Still, it seems to help Angie, and she doesn't resist when Mom starts herding her toward the front door. Mom looks back over her shoulder and says, "You go back to the party, Lisa. Angie will come out when she's ready." And I'm dismissed. I don't mind though. Mom's a lot better than I am at things like this.

Yeah, as jealous as I am of Angie having her mother's car all the time, I wouldn't want to trade places with her now.

When I get back to the patio, I see Jimmy is engrossed with something Jemmy is showing him on his tablet. I told Jemmy to stay inside while my friends were here, but of course he hasn't. I grab a couple bags of chips, go over to them and say, "Isn't it past your bed time, Jeremiah?"

He gives me a grin and a shrug.

Jimmy looks up, takes the chips I'm handing him, and says, "Have you ever seen how beautiful False Coral Snakes are? It's a shame all we have here is garter snakes. But they're beautiful too in their own way. I didn't know they were ovoviviparous, did you?"

Jemmy is nodding and hanging on Jimmy's every word like he's the Sun and the Moon. He says, "Me and Jimmy are gonna build a hiber-nacu-lum tomorrow. We're looking for instructions."

Obviously I should correct his grammar and normally I would, but two five-syllable words, undeniably nifty for that reason alone and fun to say besides? I'm not quite sure about the second one. "A hiberna...what?"

"Hibernaculum," Jemmy says it with more confidence this time. "It's a safe place for snakes to hibernate. Jimmy thinks it will attract them."

"Why would you want to attract snakes?"

"They're helpful, Lisa," Jimmy says. "They eat bugs and slugs and mice and so on."

"I know, but we have a cat for that," I point out, although of course Bitsy doesn't eat slugs. I hope. Don't get me wrong, I'm a big fan of snakes, it's just that I thought we had enough given I have to rescue them from Bitsy about ten times every summer.

But Jimmy's attention is back on the tablet. It's okay. Although he's just one grade behind me and is taking some Grade Twelve courses besides, he's only fifteen and according to Mom, he's a young fifteen at that so he's probably more comfortable with Jemmy than with the other kids. I toss the second bag of chips on the table next to Jemmy and say, "There's still lots of hot dogs."

"Thanks, Lis," Jimmy says, totally focusing on the tablet. He rips open his chips without looking at me again.

"I'll leave you to your hibernaculum research, then," I say, pleased I already got to use that word even while thinking it's unlikely I'll ever be able to use it again. I get another Coke, without rum this time since it appears there's no more sharesies. Coop is drinking straight out of the bottle now. I'm surprised it's lasted this long and wonder if there was more than one bottle.

I go to hang with Bailey and the other girls for some horse talk. I tell everyone Bailey has been working toward taking her horse to the fall show at Beban Park and she admits she's pretty excited about that. Yes, she's been to plenty of other shows before, but this time she's moving up a level so her test is more difficult.

"I hope we're ready! Our canter half pass isn't a hundred percent confirmed," she says to everyone. We all nod like a bunch of bobbleheads. I'm sure nobody but Bailey knows what a canter half pass is. She smiles, then turns to me and asks, "Are you taking Peony?"

I shake my head. "No. I just found my trot for the first time and I'm not sure I can find it again and forget canter anything, most of the time I can't even get left lead. Plus I don't have a way of getting there. Or a dressage saddle."

"Oh, that shouldn't stop you! I'll bet we have a saddle that would fit Peony, and I'm sure Mom would haul her for you. Just go in a training level test or even a walk-trot test if you don't want to canter. It would be good to get Peony out. You know, it's an important part of her education."

I won't lie, I'm gobsmacked, for two reasons: one, Peony and me, in a show? This is an opportunity I don't want to pass up. And two: Bailey and her mom would do all that for me? I say, "Wow, Bailey, really?"

"We'll all go to cheer you on," Alexis, one of the rescue volunteers "volunteers" all of them. "You too, Bailey!" she says. Now the whole group is getting in on it. "We can help you groom and all that. We'll have our own team!"

"That would be so cool!" Bailey says. This is her first time meeting the kids from the rescue and I almost didn't invite her tonight because she's older and rich besides so I thought she'd have herds of friends and not want to bother with someone like me. But she's not only fitting right in but seems happy about it.

What she's not so happy about, though, is Coop. Not that she's said anything, but I notice she keeps looking his way, and gets a cranky face each time.

Just then, the patio doors slide open and out steps Angie. I catch her eye and wave her over. "Grab a pop," I call out to her. "Wanna hot dog?"

"Just a pop," she says. She busies herself rooting through the cooler, pulls out a 7 Up and comes to stand beside me.

"You okay?" I ask quietly.

"I'm good," she says. She nods but doesn't look at me. She knows the kids from the rescue of course, but she's never met Bailey, so I introduce her.

Going by the loud eruptions of laughter, the boys are telling jokes. Angie can be a bit of a prude and the jokes are likely of the raunchy variety so I don't bother hauling her over there to introduce her to Coop right then.

As it turns out, I don't need to anyway, because in a few minutes, he breaks away from Alain and Curtis and comes waltzing right over to Angie to introduce himself.

Something sets Alain off and he starts singing "I'm a lumberjack and I'm okay". A bunch of us join in. Alain often sings this song as he works around the rescue, because he's from northern Quebec and talks about how the men in his family were all lumberjacks, so he's making fun of them and by extension, himself I guess. He claims to know all the verses but I suspect he misses some and cuts right to one about wearing panties and dresses and then adds some risqué verses of his own invention.

You guessed it, Alain is a big ham and seems to think it's his role in life to entertain everyone. His English is flawless but when he's goofing around, he lays on his most extreme French Canadian accent. He is a Good Guy and always Fun To Have Around.

The evening goes on and finally Jimmy joins the big kids, fooling around with Alain, jabbering away in French. Jimmy is pretty good at French thanks to French Immersion classes in elementary school, and he often trades sentences with Alain at the rescue, but I suspect at this moment Alain is teaching him how to swear in French. That might be a valuable thing to know so I'm paying attention. I'm not paying attention to Coop, though, until I notice he seems to be spending more time with Angie than with Bailey, he's standing way too close, and Angie looks pretty happy about it. I'm starting to feel bad for Bailey.

When they sashay around to the back of the pergola where they're out of sight thanks to the curtains bunched up there, I follow and find Coop has Angie backed up against the support post. Neither of them is glad to see me. I say, "Hey, Angie, can I talk to you for a minute?"

She gives me a frown, then pries herself away from Coop and follows me a couple of steps off. "What?" she demands.

"Angie, this isn't like you!" I hiss in an almost-whisper. "You're making Bailey feel bad."

"Not my fault he's interested."

"Umm..." I'm stunned.

"They're *not* married. He asked for my number and I gave it to him."

"But could you at least not be so obvious about it?"

"I didn't want to come in the first place, remember?" Angie says. "I told you I'd be lousy company. I'm gonna leave now." She sweeps away, giving Coop a big grin as she passes him, tossing her pop can in the recycling as she heads for her car without saying a word to anyone else.

I'm stunned! Angie of the Fine Private School Manners storming off like that? I go back to stand with Bailey.

"She's leaving?" Bailey asks as we watch her go.

"Yeah. She...uh..."

Bailey's eyes narrow and she frowns. Coop is following Angie. I try to distract her with: "Umm, what time is your lesson tomorrow?"

As if she didn't hear my question, she says, "I guess I'll leave, too, Lisa. See you at Elke's tomorrow."

"I don't have a lesson tomorrow."

"Come anyway. I'll help you. We'll start working on your test for the show. Thanks for the party."

But she doesn't follow Coop and Angie; instead, she goes into the house. I'm guessing she needs a bathroom break before grabbing Cooper and heading home, but then I see her car under the driveway lights speeding out ahead of Angie's. She couldn't have had time to go to the bathroom.

I see Coop coming back and realize Bailey left without him, avoiding him by going through the house.

Just when I think things can't get worse, Coop stumbles across the patio, barely misses the firepit, and heads for one of Mom's tall ceramic planters. He grabs it by the rim and yaks onto the little bush struggling to live there. "Yaaahhk! Yaaahhhk! Yaaa-aa-aahhk!" It seems to go on forever. No chance for anyone to miss that!

My heart sinks when I see Mom at the patio door, watching vomit drip off the shrub. Just then, Coop yells out: "Fire in the hole!" and rips a trumpet-blast of a fart. He turns around to see everyone looking his way, laughs as he takes a staggering step, and says, "Not bad for a half inch speaker, eh?"

If you needed proof being a rich kid doesn't mean you have social graces or even a brain, there you have it.

There are a few half-hearted chuckles. Coop must be the only one who didn't notice Mom. The kids from the rescue must think I have complete lowlifes for friends. Well, not lowlifes, just one lowlife because Bailey was super but even Bailey being so nice would not be enough to cancel out Coop. Just that quickly, Bailey and Coop don't seem like a good fit after all despite their both being short. I guess everyone's wondering what she's doing with him. I know I am.

It's still early, not quite midnight, but the other people start leaving, too. They're putting their empty pop cans in the recycle bin, gathering dirty paper plates, collecting chip bags and so on. Working at the rescue teaches you to tidy up and not just after yourself since the animals are pretty much slobs, except for the donkeys who like to put all their poop on one pile, which I'm sure you'll agree is very tidy.

Mom stands looking around. You'd think she'd be pleased to see everyone cleaning up but she looks like she has something awful tasting in her mouth. I guess that whole yakking thing right onto her pampered Rose of Sharon even without the fart is difficult to overlook. I wonder about suggesting a liter of rum-soaked hot dogs and chips might be good fertilizer but think better of it.

Jimmy is staying over so with any luck the talking to I'm sure to get will be postponed until he goes home and by then, Mom shouldn't be quite as furious as she looks right now. Then again, Jimmy stays over so often we call the guest room Jimmy's room, so him being here might not be a deterrent.

Fortunately Alain offers to give Coop a ride home. Coop has already puked so chances are reasonably good he won't hurl in Alain's car. Alain smiles back over his shoulder at me as he herds Coop out to where his car is parked.

When Jimmy and I bring the food leftovers into the kitchen, Mom and Dad are not in evidence. I've been reprieved! My relief is short-lived though because judging by the sounds coming from the master bedroom, they're discussing something. I have no doubt it's my choice of friends or Coop in particular. Based on how loud they are, I'm guessing it's a spirited discussion. They must be at odds as to what, if anything, should be done. As if they needed something else to argue about! I feel terrible to be the cause.

ANGIE, JIMMY AND I have our shift at the Mid-Island Horse and Donkey Rescue every Sunday afternoon, but this morning, Angie's not answering my texts or phone. I hope it's because she's embarrassed and doesn't want to face us after her behavior at the party. Mom gives Jimmy and me a ride.

I see Alain busy on Poo Picking Detail and give him a wave.

"Hey," he calls out, "thanks for the party! It was a good time!"

I think he means it. Maybe the party wasn't such a disaster after all. I can't help myself, I have to ask, "Did Coop throw up in your car?"

"No. He said he felt sick so I stopped and let him get out so he could puke on someone else's shrubs. Pissed himself while he was at it."

I'm surprised Coop was coherent enough to give him that much warning and double triple glad he didn't pee his pants when Bailey could see it. Or maybe it would be a good thing if she did.

If you're wondering, Angie was a no show.

Nikki and Jackson

IT'S A LOVELY EVENING for a stroll but Nikki isn't enjoying it. She spent most of the day at the beach. She's covered in sunblock and sand. Her feet hurt and she still has an hour's walk. To top it all off, now that the sun is setting the mosquitoes are coming out. It was a crappy thing to do and she still can't believe they did it to her.

She's not used to walking, so she's tiring. It's almost more than she can manage to keep putting one foot in front of the other. She begins counting, "One, two, three, four" and so on. When she gets to a hundred, she begins at one again. When she gets to a hundred for the second time, she says, "Two hundred," and begins at one again.

An unpleasant, pungent smell assaults her. There seems to be something rustling around in the underbrush next to the path just behind her. She stops and turns around to see what it is. The branches on the low shrubbery move a little as if stirred by a breeze, then are still, and the bad smell fades.

"What was that?" she asks of no one. There's no breeze so why did the branches rustle? She stands statue-still watching that spot in the bushes to see if one of the feral rabbits that live everywhere around here might come out. Or maybe it was birds.

But all is quiet except for the steady hum of the traffic on the nearby freeway, and the bushes remain still. She thinks she must have been imagining things or whatever was in the bush is long gone. She continues on her way. But she's lost count of her steps, so she gives up counting, turns on her iPhone playlist and puts her earbuds on.

It's getting late and she feels an uneasy twinge of nerves when she realizes if she doesn't speed it up, she won't get through the part of the path that goes through the forest before it's dark.

The bushes next to the path just a few meters ahead move; she stops in her tracks again, and watches. It's something bigger than a rabbit. There have been bear and cougar sightings here! More likely, it's a deer. She draws a deep breath. That smell again! The branches are still. All is quiet. But she is filled with the feeling of being watched and the hairs on the back of her neck prickle. She begins singing along with Taylor Swift, loudly but tunelessly, and walks faster.

As she comes to the beginning of the forest she starts jogging. This isn't easy in flip flops, and she mutters, "God damn you all to hell, Lily Mae!"

Tears sting her eyes when she thinks about the other girls leaving the beach while she was in the ladies room. They had done the same thing to others before, but Nikki never thought Lily Mae would do it to her!

The first time they took off on someone was last fall. They were watching the boys show off at the skate bowl. Lauren was on the other side fooling around with Jackson, and when the two of them went down the path that leads behind the skate bowl and out of sight, Lily

Mae said, "Let's take off on her!" They bolted for the car, jumped in, and went racing out of the parking lot, spewing gravel. It was thrilling! They laughed so hard they cried, thinking how shocked Lauren would be when she finally took her eyes off Jackson and realized they had left. Payback for her coming on to Jackson. Everyone knows he's Lily Mae's boyfriend! At least Lauren had a chance to get a ride home because Jackson and some other guys were still skating.

But she never got home. Jackson said she hadn't wanted to wait until he was ready to go so she started off hitching and hasn't been seen since. Foolish girl! Everyone knows hitching is dangerous anytime, but around here? Where so many girls have disappeared?

Today, Lily Mae and the new girl left when they were the last people at the beach and it was already nearly dark. Lily Mae knew it would mean she had no way to get home other than to walk. She not only didn't care, but planned it. It would be a nasty thing to do any time, but especially with all the missing girls!

Nikki is breathing too hard to sing now and can't run anymore. The smell is stronger here and she identifies it as sewage. Kind of smoky sewage. She wishes she could hold her breath. *There must be a sewer pipe running through here, and it's broken,* she thinks. Or maybe it's just that the level of water in the swamp is higher than usual because of the rainy summer.

The forest is not only dark but feels ten degrees colder. An intense chill knifes through her and she wishes she had more than the flimsy cover-up over her bikini. A big sweatshirt like those worn by girls who have no boobs to show off would be welcome now.

Worse, the feeling of being watched has intensified and several times she's so sure she's being followed she looks over her shoulder. She stops and turns on the flashlight on her iPhone. The low battery warning flashes on the screen. She has to get through the forest before it goes out! Her guts clench.

"It's not much further," she tells herself, "You're halfway there!" Once out into the open stretch next to the highway she'll be safe.

Something catches her toe and she sprawls forward, landing painfully on hands and knees. She jumps to her feet. The heels of her hands and both knees are scraped. Burning. Stinging. She picks up her phone but just as she does, the battery dies. No more flashlight! It's enough to make her cry but she tells herself, *nothing's broken, get moving.* She gives an anguished sob and walks on, more slowly now, desperate to stay on the path. Branches seem to be reaching out to grab her and something, likely a blackberry vine, nearly wraps around her arm. It scratches painfully as she pulls her arm free.

Suddenly a dark figure steps out of the gloom right in front of her. He is dressed all in black with a hood up over his head. His face is so deep inside the hood he appears faceless. She screams.

"Nikki!" the figure says, "Did I scare you? I'm sorry." He pushes his hood back and Nikki recognizes him.

"Jackson! Yeah, you scared me! Scared the shit outta me, actually!" Nikki takes a few deep breaths to calm herself, then walks up to him. "What are you doing here?"

"Lily Mae told me what, er, happened at the lake. It was a joke, she said. She has a rotten sense of humour sometimes."

"Ya think? So...You came to find me?"

"Yeah."

"My hero!"

"That's me! My car's parked up at the storage lot. I thought I could intercept you here and give you a ride the rest of the way."

"Oh, that's great. But the storage lot? It's quite a walk still."

"There's a shortcut through the bush. The trail starts here." He turns and indicates a break in the underbrush.

"Oh! Okay," Nikki says. It's not much of a trail, but it does explain how Jackson was able to materialize on the path right in front of her, seemingly out of thin air. She falls in behind him as he leads her into the deeper gloom off the main path.

"I can't see a thing! Don't you have a flashlight? At least your phone?"

"It's okay, I have really good night vision. Like a cat!"

Did his eyes suddenly flash? Nikki is reminded of her cat's eyes: golden, with the pupil a vertical slit. But she must have been imagining things. He did say cat, after all. That must have tricked her brain.

"Just stay with me. Here, take my hand." His eyes are perfectly normal as he offers his hand. She clasps it and feels a vast sense of relief as she allows him to tow her along.

It's so dark she can't see where she's going, but Jackson goes on without hesitation. She thinks, *he really does have cat-like vision.* She's so close she can smell him. It's a scent of smoke and sweat, masculine but rather unpleasant. She'll have to ask him what cologne he's wearing and suggest he get something else.

Just as Nikki has that thought Jackson stops so abruptly she bumps into him, and steps right out of her flip flop.

"Aggghh! A little warning would be nice! I've lost my flip flop and I now can't see where it is. What did you stop for?"

There's movement in the underbrush a several meters off the narrow path, much more powerful than the rustling noises Nikki noticed earlier. She screams.

"It's okay," Jackson says, and pulls her roughly into his arms. "It's my, er, cousin."

"Cousin?" When she has fantasized about being in his arms she thought it would be nice, but he's holding her as if she'll get away, and not gently. "Jeez, Jackson, not so tight!"

The underbrush rustles as though a powerful whirlwind is passing through and a funnel cloud of tiny swirling stars forms. As it comes closer, the stars coalesce, becoming more and more solid until they form a creature. Covered with glistening scales, it looms up over them, staring with the lidless black eyes of a snake. Flaps like small, jagged elephant ears run up the sides of its face, joined together by a glowing green ridge across the top of its head, illuminating a sphere around them. There are two holes that must be nostrils, and the drooling, red-rimmed mouth has double rows of long teeth. Rope-thin forelegs undulate as the creature's body sways like a snake charmer's cobra. There are long, sabre-like claws on its hands? paws? but the appendages appear useless.

This is Jackson's cousin? Nikki can't suppress a sobbing squeak; she shrinks back and tries to hide behind Jackson, but he turns her to face the creature, his hands like vice grips on her arms.

"Very good, Jacksssssson! Thissss issss a nissssss one," the creature hisses. Plumes of smoke come from its nostrils.

"This is the last one I'm gonna bring you," Jackson says.

"Thissss issss not your choissss."

"The cops are starting to get suspicious. You've seen them going all through here with their dogsss, right? They're hunting ussss!"

"You hafff to be more careffffulll."

"No! I'm done! I've changed my mind. I don't want immortality, or magic. I don't want to live in the sssssswamp..."

"You don't hafff a choisss."

"No! I'm not gonna do it! I won't be a ffffreak like you! I..."

With astonishing speed, one of the creature's little arms slices the air. A sabre-like claw slashes Jackson's neck. His head falls and rolls across Nikki's feet as she's covered in hot arterial blood spray.

She has time to think, *oh, those arms aren't useless after all.*

It's strange how the mind works.

Then the creature enfolds her and her nostrils fill with the choking, nauseating stench of smoke and sewage as she's pulled against him. She isn't able to utter more than a squawk before it bites through her neck.

The creature picks up Jackson's body. Everything disintegrates into a swirling mist of tiny stars and disappears.

CALL ME LISA

IN THE MORNING, ALL that is found is a torn, discarded flip flop, and of course, Jackson's head. Instead of skin on the back of his neck there are shiny, iridescent scales. His grieving parents explain that the family is cursed with a rare form of psoriasis that affects a few unfortunate individuals every other generation. To respect the family's wishes, this detail is never disclosed to the media.

AND THAT IS THE STORY of how I lost my two friends. Didn't see that coming, did you?

I'll have to wait until the last class of the creative writing course to find out if Mrs. Wiebe liked it. I think *Nikki and Jackson* is a very Stephen King-ish story, and I hope Mrs. Wiebe agrees because that's what I was going for. He has been my all-time most favourite writer since I read *Carrie*. I think that might be the first book he wrote. Of course he's written about a hundred since. I got *Carrie* at a book sale and I always look for other Stephen King books at thrift stores, so I've added quite a few to my collection.

It's important for an aspiring author to do a lot of reading, all genres, and I've started my own library. You can do this even on a small budget by getting books at book sales and thrift stores as I've mentioned I've done. I also have books by my other all time, most favourite writers: Margaret Atwood, Anne Rice, Larry McMurtry, J.K. Rowling and so on.

Is it nice to imagine horrible deaths for people just because they've been awful to you? Maybe not. But it makes me feel better and really, they were dead to me before I wrote this.

You should keep in mind that it's never a good idea to screw over a writer, because you will only have yourself to blame if you are killed off in their next story.

Back to School

IT HARDLY SEEMS POSSIBLE summer vacation could be over, but here I am, back in the Halls of Learning. My locker assignment is on the ground floor this year, which is nice since it means I won't have to go up and down the stairs all the time like last year. Just through the front doors, left turn, past the office and library and boom! My locker. A real time saver. But now Jimmy's locker is on the top floor and I'll be running up and down to see him so I haven't really gained anything. Maybe it's a good thing, because Mom says about fifteen times a day she needs steps and if she needs them probably I do too.

I have no way of knowing how many steps I have or still need. Mom has this fancy watch called a FitBit that keeps track of her steps and she's mentioned a few times I should have one, I would love it and so on. I don't know why I need one because I'm always stepping, back and forth to the barn, doing chores and so on, so I'm probably getting plenty of steps. It is true I'm not getting as many since I got my laptop and have been spending so much time writing stories, though, so I'm sure Mom has my best interests at heart. Still, I really want a dressage saddle and she seems to miss subtle hints such as "I'd rather have the money to put towards my saddle", so I suspect I'll probably get a FitBit for Christmas or my birthday. Knowing this ahead of time gives me a chance to practice being surprised. It won't kill me and might even be good for me, exercise being important for your health as I'm sure you know.

You might be wondering why I need a new saddle, because Bailey said I could use one of hers. Didn't she come through on that offer?

High Five to you for pointing that out, and yes, she loaned me a dressage saddle. I've been using it all week. The good thing about going from western to dressage rather than to jumping is that your legs are still long and you sit up tall instead of hunching over so it's not a big change that way.

I'm starting to feel really cool now that I've figured out which diagonal to rise on. Actually, I'll admit it, I first had to learn what a diagonal *is*. Turns out at trot horses move their legs in diagonal pairs, right front with left hind and vice versa. It's so basic even the little kids Elke teaches know their diagonals so I felt like an idiot asking about it, but Elke says no question is a stupid question and keeps telling me what I'm doing right now is the most difficult part of becoming a Dressage Rider. Even Marci and Bailey and World Champions like Charlotte Dujardin spend a lot of their lessons working on basics, she says. I'm pretty sure she's just saying that so I don't get discouraged. I've watched Bailey's lesson and haven't heard Elke telling her to shorten up her reins, sit up straight and check her diagonal fifteen times every minute.

Anyway. The saddle. It's a really nice one and Marci has offered to sell it to me. Even though she paid more than five thousand dollars for it so it's a good deal at three thousand, it is still way, way *WAY* out of my price range. I'm hoping to find a used one for a lot less. I'm watching for one at our local tack shops and on Kijiji and Garage Sale and so on, and so are Elke and Bailey and Marci and everyone so I should be able to get one soon.

I can't keep using this expensive saddle! I'm worried I'll do something dumb and damage it. To that end, I always clean it, put the cover on, and put it away carefully after every ride which is just a good thing to do for any saddle, even your own. I also wash the pad Bailey loaned me every time I use it because we dressage riders always start with a clean one. (Knowing this now, I'm mildly embarrassed at my treatment of my western saddle. You should see the girth, or what on a western saddle is called the cinch, not to mention the pad.)

FYI, Elke loves Peony! She says she will make a fine dressage horse and thinks she's pretty even with her missing eye. So with help finding a saddle and how much she likes Peony you can see why I like Elke so much. Not just Elke but everyone at the barn and of course especially Bailey.

Anyway. I'm at school, getting my locker organized. I have one of those locker organizers on the inside of the door, you know the type: one side is a little basket for holding pens or I guess lipstick if I wore it, and the other side is a mirror. The mirror is plastic so you don't have to worry about breaking it, but it's marginal as far as mirrors go as it makes you look like on TV when they blur the faces to Protect The Innocent.

Regarding lipstick. I know you're thinking: don't most girls wear it by the time they're in Grade Twelve? High Five to you, yes, they do. I've tried it of course, but I guess I'm not careful enough because I end up getting it on everything: my collar, my cuff, the sleeve of my jacket and even my teeth. I don't like what I look like with red lips anyway. With my red hair and big feet, if you add big red lips I look like Ronald McDonald even though I don't have red shoes. I do wear eyeshadow and mascara and some foundation to tone down my freckles, though. You know, stuff you don't have to touch up during the day. It's enough trouble remembering not to rub my eyes and smear all that without worrying about my lips.

In other words, I don't really need the mirror/bin thing but Jemmy got it for me. It was so thoughtful I made a big fuss thanking him. He may have regretted giving it to me, judging by how he squirmed when I bear-hugged him and kissed his face even though as I mentioned I don't wear lipstick so it's not like he needed to wash his face after. He did anyway. I guess he's at that Hate Girl Germs age. Like not making constant noise, not wanting to be hugged is another sign he's not a little kid anymore.

Anyway. There are new faces in the halls but the same old faces are still here too. Some I really wish weren't, like Laurie Ann Reedy and The Coven. I hoped with the drug bust last year they would have scattered to the winds but nope, they're still a unit and still to be avoided.

They haven't forgotten their nicknames for me: Geronimo (I have no idea what that's about), Lister (the boy version of Lisa?) so like Lister-een why don't you use your mouthwash and so on, and the always popular Stretch and Too Tall (no explanation needed). This year they've come up with a new one: Lesbo. Clever, no? If you don't wear enough makeup or gawdy jewelry, or if you prefer jeans and sweaters to short skirts and low-cut shirts and if you tend to be a little flat-chested, you're obviously a lesbian, right? It's about time people quit caring about a person's sexual orientation, in my opinion.

Over summer they all got tattoos on the inside of their left wrists. I haven't had a good look but I hear from others it's something Laurie Ann designed and believe it or not, it's her initials all jazzed up with flowers. I can't imagine how she convinced them it was a good idea to permanently mark themselves with someone else's initials. I guess they had no choice, it was something they had to do if they wanted to be her friend, so called. It's a cult mentality and rather than sickening, it's sad. I've noticed Nicole has one, so it looks like she's a Full Patch Member or Full Tattoo Member of The Coven now. Good thing she dumped me as a friend or who knows, I might have been sucked into that. After hearing about the Rye Drinking Incident I imagine you understand.

Anyway. To bring you up to date: I'm the one who ratted them out about the drugs and while I was at it I reported the bullying. Although it was months ago, I doubt anyone has forgotten and I worry about retribution. I've promised to report any bullying to Mr. Dvorak, our principal, but I guess time will reveal two things: one, if there will be a repeat of anything such as Stealing Jimmy's Homework or the Pushing Lisa Down Incident; and two: if I would actually go through with tattling about it again. It might make things worse. There are so many places they could get me alone far from prying eyes such as the forested part of the trail, even though there is no swamp creature, if they want to go that far.

You might think it's crazy to worry about things like that and I'm just paranoid, but they got pretty nasty last year what with the Pushing Down Incident I mentioned. But when I give it more thought I realize they would never jump me at the forested part of the trail because they'd have to walk quite a distance to get to it and they wouldn't go to that much trouble. More likely if they decide to do something it will be at school. Which is not to say I will like it any better.

"Hey," Angie says as she materializes beside me.

"Hey," I respond. I'm finished getting my books for the morning's classes so I shut the door and close the lock. "What's up?"

"Dad got home last night."

"Well, that's good."

"Yeah, it's good. He says he won't be going out of town again."

"Double good!"

"So, I have the car, and I don't have to hurry home right after school. I thought we could go over to Bellissimo Ink and get tattoos on our wrists."

"*What?*"

"Yeah. I thought we could work our initials into the flowers..."

"Have you lost your mind?"

"I'm kidding, Lis! Jeez!"

I give a big sigh of relief. This is more like the old Angie. Well, the new old Angie. When we first started hanging out, she was serious and not only didn't joke about anything but she also didn't get it when I was joking. I liked her anyway because despite not having a sense of humour, she is a very good person, but I like her a lot better since she has lightened up. She goes more for subtle jokes such as pretending we would get tattoos like The Coven's whereas I go in more for slapstick/stupid stuff like going cross-eyed or hanging a spoon on my nose. Although it's showing off, hanging a spoon on your nose is a skill and any skills you have are worth capitalizing on, in my opinion.

Maybe being raised by two stuffy old people accounts for Angie's somber world view. You might be surprised to learn her mom being old and sick has one benefit: she often doesn't feel up to driving, so being sick is the reason Angie almost always has her car.

As much as I've envied Angie having the car and credit card, Angie envies me having my Mom who not only isn't sick but who she thinks is cool. Witness the fact she didn't ream me out for Coop's behavior, you know, the booze and so on, although she has mentioned there won't be another party for a while. If you're wondering, the Rose of Sharon seems fine, so a moratorium on parties is harsh punishment, in my opinion. Also pointless, since that was the first party I had since my tenth birthday and I have no plans to up the party schedule.

"Anyway," Angie continues as we walk toward home room, "I wouldn't get them on my wrist. I'm thinking of my left boob."

I laugh.

She gives me a sharp look. This time she's not kidding. I give her a sharp look right back in hopes I won't have to tell her what a stupid idea I think that is, but she just shrugs it off. I say, "I never thought you'd want to be a non-conformist like everyone else."

That floated right over her head and flew away, obviously, because she looked at me with a frown and said, "A non-conformist *isn't* like everyone else."

Well, *duh!*

Speaking of Angie, you're probably wondering about the Coop thing. There have been developments on that front. I didn't know if I should tell Bailey he asked Angie for her number. I decided it might be just drunk talk and he wouldn't follow through on it so no harm done, really, and I'd stay out of it. Then a few days later, Angie and I were planning on shopping for school things, and she cancelled. Reason: she had a date with Coop. If you remember, at the party I told Angie her paying attention to Coop bothered Bailey, but she didn't care. The next time I saw her I told her about the Rose of Sharon and Trumpet Blast Incident thinking that would really turn her off, but she thought it was funny. I guess maybe it was, and I'm just being judgmental because I didn't like what he did to Bailey.

I really didn't know what to do. Coop and Bailey have been together for almost a year. Sure, they're not married, but if they haven't split up and he's sneaking around, it's a lousy thing to do. I decided to tell Bailey. She confronted him and they split.

I still wonder if I did the right thing, telling Bailey. You know, hurt one friend even if it makes the other one happy? But it's done. For Angie, the coast is clear. Maybe he's a good guy when he's not drunk, but I don't think that's the case because a good guy would never have asked Angie out without first breaking up with Bailey. I know it happens all the time, but it's dishonest. Put that with the drinking and farting, and nobody deserves a creep like Coop for a boyfriend in my opinion. But Angie doesn't see anything wrong with him and constantly mentions how handsome he is and how rich, as if that makes it okay. It's awkward between her and me now so we don't talk about it.

It was out of character for me to say something to her at the party in the first place as I always avoid confrontation and/or uncomfortable situations. I guess not talking about it since is me being me.

ONE OF THE PEOPLE FROM last year that's back again is, you guessed it, my old friend Jarrett. I have mixed feelings about that because he turned into such a jerk when he started dating Laurie Ann. It looks like she dumped him or at least they split over summer, because I haven't seen them together.

Even though Jarrett has broken free of Laurie Ann's Force Field Containment Spell, I thought being her boyfriend even if it was for just a few months would mean he'd have no trouble getting another girlfriend from The Coven or some other popular group I'm not a member of, so I'm surprised when on Monday morning, I see movement in the squiggly mirror on my locker door and turn to find Jarrett beside me.

"Hi, Lisa," he says.

It feels like my eyebrows might crash into my hairline. I force them back down where they belong and crease my forehead into a frown but otherwise ignore him.

He continues: "What're you doin'?"

"Putting my books away and getting my lunch, what does it look like?"

If you're thinking that's rude and maybe I should be more polite, remember, Jarrett and I have history. The first few years we were good friends, then he started dating Laurie Ann and went over to The Dark Side. She got mad if he talked to me or even texted me and he wouldn't stand up to her so that was the end of us being friends.

The last time we spoke to each other was way last spring when he backed me up against the lockers and bellowed at me like a mad bull. He was so close and was spewing so much spittle I had to wipe my face when he finally left me alone. Ewww, right? And all because of Laurie Ann. So you can see why I mentioned losing Jarrett as a friend was a whole 'nother story and you can understand why I killed him off, figuratively. You wouldn't forgive him either, would you? And just so you know, them splitting up had nothing to do with anything I did because they had long since stopped even noticing me. I'm an Untouchable, after all.

"Grab your lunch and come with me. I'll take you for a ride in my new car," he says. He's got that 'I'm sexy and I know it' grin but otherwise looks serious.

I look around to see if any members of The Coven or maybe Jarrett's buddies are hanging around watching, ready to laugh when he does something to make me look stupid. I don't know what that might be, exactly, but you know what I mean, like when you point to a pretend spot on someone's shirt and when they look down, you tap their nose. Or you pat their back and stick a "Kick Me" note on them without them noticing. But I see nobody except the usual kids. Even so, I'll be wary should he try to pat my back.

I shake my head and turn away. This is where I should make a dramatic exit like trotting up the stairs and losing him in the lava flow of students, but the lunchroom is on the main floor, the staircase is way at the other end of the hall, and there aren't enough people still hanging around to form even a small lava flow. There's no escape. He hovers around like a bad smell even though my back is to him, then slides around behind me and holds the locker door so I can't close it.

"Hey, Lisa," he starts up again, "about, you know, before. I'm sorry."

I snort. I don't mean to, it just happens sometimes. But in this case at least it was appropriate and gets my point across. I just wish I had a Kleenex. I pass the back of my hand across my upper lip like it's itchy or something and make a mental note to get a pack of Kleenex for my locker.

"I mean it, Lisa. Really." He creases his forehead so his eyebrows kind of go up in the middle and nearly join, he's that sincere. Sure. "In fact," he continues, "leave your lunch, we'll go to the McDonalds drive-through, my treat."

"I'm having lunch with *friends*," I tell him. I've finished piling my books in my locker so I grab my lunch bag, pull the door to release it from his meat hook and slam it.

"How about after school, then?"

I wave him off and head for the lunch room. Thankfully he doesn't follow.

I'm upset; not in a bad way exactly, just in a mixed-emotions way. I miss Jarrett, but I've made new friends and I'm getting along without him just fine. Also, I don't know if I can trust Remorseful Jarrett even though he did look sheepish and maybe even humbled. We were friends for a long time, and a person can't have too many friends, can they? If so, what's the recommended upper limit? If it's more than half a dozen, I don't have to worry.

I get to the lunchroom and spot Angie and Jimmy, saving a place for me at the farthest table, so I join them. I've come in at the middle of Angie telling Jimmy about her plan for a tattoo on her boob.

"Yeah, so I thought I'd get a little cluster of violas over my heart. That's Mom's favourite flower."

"Sure," Jimmy says, "that would be really nice. You know, a tribute or, er..."

"Jimmy!" I exclaim, "don't encourage her! Think about what those flowers will look like when everything starts to sag!"

"They won't sag much FFS and besides, that won't be for a long time," Angie says. "Everyone's got tattoos. You're just so, umm, out of it, Lisa! Besides, no one's ever going to see it." As she shoves half her sandwich to Jimmy, she gives me a stink eye.

She has that look down pat and it's always daunting. I've tried but I can't do it as well as she does, I just come off looking like I've gone off my meds. My signature go-to move instead of stink eye, when it's really needed, is to stick out my tongue but I've mostly quit doing that as I've been told a number of times it's childish. So I quit arguing, shrug and say, "So you're never going to wear a bikini? And what's the point if no one's even going to know you have it?"

"You wouldn't understand."

"You're right, I don't. But I guess it's your boob and you can do with it what you wish."

"Exactly," she agrees. "I've gone through Bellisimo's book. They have hundreds of pictures of beautiful tattoos. You should see it, Lisa! I think you'd change your mind, you being an artist and all. But I haven't found what I'm looking for, so I was hoping you would design something for me."

As much as I should point out I'm no longer an artist but a writer, which I'm surprised she's forgotten, and I don't want to be a party to what I think is a stupid thing to do, I say, "I'll give it a shot." It's a hollow promise as I have no intention of doing it, but if it becomes an issue, a bunch of flowers is dead easy to draw. If worse comes to worse I can trace something out of Mom's adult coloring book.

I pull out my all time, most favourite sandwich: peanut butter and dill pickle on multigrain, unwrap it and dig in. I've finished my sandwich and I'm peeling my orange when I remember I didn't see Angie earlier this morning and haven't heard how her mom is doing. She seems so chipper I think asking will be okay. "By the way, how is your Mom, Angie?"

"Pretty good. She was at the cancer clinic Friday. Looks like she may be in remission. She was up and about a few times over the week-end. We went to Milano's for dinner Sunday."

"Oh, that's great!" I give a big sigh, for three reasons: one, Angie's mom being in remission is news anyone can understand is great; two, there was at least one day or part of a day she didn't spend with Coop; and three, Milano's makes a great moussaka. There is even a vegetarian option although no vegan version, owing to the bechamel topping which I imagine would be hard to make without eggs and milk. If you're wondering, when we go to Milano's, I happily eat the vegetarian moussaka, bechamel or not. "Did you have moussaka?"

"What do you think?"

"Mmmmm! Moussaka!" I've almost forgotten about Jarrett when I see Laurie Ann and a couple of the other Coven members come into the lunch room and sit at the next table. The sight of them reminds me.

"Hey guys!" I say in an almost-whisper, "You won't believe what happened just before I came in here!"

"What?" Jimmy asks. Angie just looks at me because she's in mid-chew. She has fine manners so she won't speak with her mouth full.

"Jarrett came to my locker and said he was sorry. Even said he'd treat me to lunch at McDonalds because he has a car now."

"What?" Angie blurts out, food-in-mouth be damned. She nearly chokes, but recovers and after she calms herself, says, "Well, I think I knew about his car, saw him getting into it one day, but umm, he actually apologized? What did you tell him?"

"I said I was having lunch with friends, heavy emphasis on *friends*."

"What brought this on? Does he really think since Laurie Ann dumped him he can just come crawling back to you and you'll welcome him with open arms?"

"First of all, are we sure she dumped him?'

"*He* might have dumped *her*," Jimmy points out.

"Dump*ee* or dump*er*, I'm not sure there's been a dump at all. I haven't seen them together but that could just be part of their evil design. And besides, you know it's not like that with Jarrett and me. It never *was* like that. We were never boyfriend-girlfriend, just friends."

"Oh yeah, I remember now, and that kissing practice you told me about was just what friends do."

"Pretty much. And keep your voice down!"

The skinny guy in a camo T-shirt sitting next to Angie looks right at me so I know he's listening. I feel heat rising to my face. Do I want anyone to know about Kissing Practice? I'm sorry I told Angie about it.

"Friends with benefits?" Jimmy asks, looking at me with those brown eyes appearing twice their actual size thanks to his glasses. As if that's going to prompt me to fill in details!

"God no! Anyway, it was a long time ago," I say, "and I told you that in confidence, big mouth!"

"Sorry!" Angie says, "I didn't know it was a big deal! And I think a lot of girls would like to have a few practice sessions kissing Jarrett. You'd be the envy of the graduating class! If you haven't noticed, he's a hunk."

"I haven't noticed." Of course I have, it's just that it wasn't front of mind. He's always just been Jarrett to me. I spend a few seconds thinking about him and realize he's grown over summer so he's now taller than I am and he must be working out because he's got muscles where he never had any before. But my face still feels hot, so to divert attention, I say to Angie, "But since you've obviously been gawking, want me to introduce you?"

"Sure!" she agrees so quickly it's my turn to choke.

"What? What about Coop?"

"He, umm, that didn't amount to anything," she says. She's not prone to blushing owing to her darker skin, but if not for that I think she would be red in the face. As if she's uncomfortable, she rushes on: "Next time Jarrett talks to you, invite him to your place and I'll show up too."

"Wait a minute! You and Coop didn't amount to anything? After you going on and on about *he's so handsome* and *he's got such a nice car* and *he's rich*?"

"Yeah, he's all of those things. But that's not why I liked him."

"Oh? You liked him because he can blast out treble farts and piss his pants? All these fine attributes and now it didn't amount to anything?"

"Oh, here comes Lisa Libra! We just didn't hit it off."

I can't help but grimace. Calling me Lisa Libra isn't as mean as Lesbo, but it's her way of telling me she thinks I'm judgmental. Harsh criticism and unwarranted, in my opinion. But I push my bruised feelings aside and ask, "So you put Bailey through all that and now you just didn't hit it off? Who are you?"

"So what, that wasn't my fault, and anyway he got back with Bailey."

Well, that explains why I didn't see Bailey over the week-end.

"About Jarrett?" Angie prompts.

"Jarrett is totally NOT going to talk to me again, wait and see. I'm sure it was just something he just did on a dare, to suck me in so he could do something to make me look like a loser."

"You don't know that!"

"I do know that."

"What he did before was just because of Laurie Ann. And I'm sure they've split otherwise why haven't we seen them hanging on each other? They split. So maybe he's on the outs with the whole group and is looking for friends again."

"And maybe he really is sorry," Jimmy chimes in.

"Okay you two! First both of you are against me on the Tattoo Issue and now on the Jarrett Issue too?"

"Yes," Angie says, "you're out-voted on both. So. Introduce me to Jarrett?"

"Okay. If you're sure."

"I'm sure."

"I wanna be in on this too," Jimmy says.

"Of course you do. Is there anyone else we should invite?"

"Who else would we invite?" Angie asks.

It's on the tip of my tongue to say something like *no one, that's the point*, or even, *no one, dummy!* I'm that irritated with her. She should notice I'm not comfortable with the whole idea and tell me to forget it because she was just teasing. But she doesn't.

At least it's not like I'll be going it alone, not the meeting part anyway, just the part where I have to invite him, and that might never happen. The good thing about agreeing to do something off in the future such as designing a stupid tattoo or setting up this stupid meeting is that you get the kudos now and may never actually have to do it.

"Just remember," I tell her, "he probably won't speak to me again."

"We could walk around until we bump into him. We must have some idea where his locker is. And I think I'd recognize his car..."

"I am *totally* not going to do that! Anyway, I still think it was some kind of joke."

"And I think you're wrong. You've been wrong before." Angie looks smug as she sticks the straw in her juice box without squeezing any juice out. That's something I'm seldom able to do, so it's a good reason to be smug, in my opinion, although I don't think that's it.

I'm about to ask who I was wrong about when a huge guffaw erupts from The Coven. Jimmy and I look up and see they're gawking at us. They're chittering like a bunch of monkeys, give us the Middle Finger Salute and start throwing feces.

Naturally Jimmy and I return the favour. The salute, not the feces-throwing which I'm sure I don't have to tell you was all in my mind. You know, because they reminded me of monkeys.

Angie is sitting with her back to them and doesn't know why we did that. She's not the kind of person who would flip the bird anyway, not even if provoked. "What are you doing?" she demands to know.

I think she'll make a fine strict parent or teacher someday because she has that tone of voice mastered.

"They did it first," Jimmy says.

"And you don't think Jarrett inviting me for lunch was a set up?" I ask. My turn to be smug.

A FEW MINUTES LATER, I get a text from Mom. I think she's probably going to want me to start dinner, peel potatoes, make a salad or something. She doesn't. She says she's not coming home until the week-end and she'll talk to Jemmy and me then. This is odd, because she said this morning she was working from home all week and she always knows her schedule ahead of time.

And "talk to you and Jemmy"? She usually says "CU". It's probably nothing. I push it out of my mind and realize it goes without saying dinner is going to be up to me for the rest of the week. If left to Dad, he'd either order pizza smothered in every kind of meat imaginable or pick up a bucket of chicken every night or put hamburgers or sausages or steaks on the barbeque. If he does that, okay, I'll make salad or whatever to go along with it. I also know how to make vegan chili and a batch of that lasts days, so maybe that's what I'll do.

Hurricane

THIN GRAY LIGHT OOZES though my window and I'm annoyed at myself for not closing the blinds before I went to bed last night. It's Saturday. I have nothing to get up early for, since my lesson isn't until ten thirty. I check my alarm clock. It's ten past six. I could sleep for another hour. Bitsy yawns and stretches. I do the same. I squeeze my eyes shut in hopes I can fall back to sleep, but after a few minutes, I realize I can't and I might as well get up.

I look out my window to see where Peony is and spy her at the end of the pasture, poking her head in one of the apple trees. She's been picking apples ever since they were small and green, and now keeps the windfalls cleaned up. If there aren't enough, such as lately because they're almost done for the year, she brings more down by grabbing a branch and giving it a shake. There's a smart horse for you! But not smart enough to stay out of the mud puddles. Judging by the big areas where she's black instead of brown, she found a good one to roll in.

The door to Mom and Dad's room is open and as I go by I notice neither of them is in bed. It's not surprising Mom isn't there; she's always Up With The Birds as Dad says, but on weekends Dad likes to sleep in. Well, at least past six. Can't blame him for that!

Mom wasn't home yet when I went to bed last night so I don't know how late it was when she got here. When I come into the kitchen, I find Mom and Dad both perched on stools at the island, one at each end. Mom is gazing out the window as she sips her coffee, her back to Dad. Dad has a mug in one hand and his phone in the other. This would be a typical morning if it was an hour later.

CALL ME LISA

"Good morning," I say, and head for the coffee maker.

"Good morning," they both mutter.

"You're up early."

Neither of them comments, so I carry on: "Peony's paddock still hasn't dried up. It's one big mud puddle. Can't we get more gravel in there, Dad? Or hog fuel maybe?"

"It dries up pretty quick," Dad says.

"Well, it's been three days since it rained and it hasn't dried up yet." I put a pod in the coffeemaker and hit brew. Mom is having her coffee black this morning I guess, because she doesn't have the Cinnaswirl out. I get it from the fridge, and when my coffee is brewed, pour some in and take a stool between them at the island. I'll have a few pieces of toast before I get dressed and go out to the barn, but not until my second cup of coffee.

"Want some help cleaning up branches before you start on the lawn, Dad?" I ask. A lot fell this week because of the rain storm and no one has been out to clean them up yet. I don't mind doing it and just offering should get me some Brownie Points. I'm sure you know how important those are and how hard they can be to come by.

"Umm, sure," Dad says. I'm puzzled at his lack of enthusiasm. When was the last time I offered to help with yard work? This doesn't bode well for Brownie Points.

Mom gives me an odd look, lifts her cup in both hands and takes a couple of sips before saying quietly, "I—we—have something important to talk to you about, Lisa. You and Jemmy."

She doesn't elaborate but looks very serious. No smiles from my usually smiling mother? Something tells me I'm not going to like this important thing and for a second my flight response kicks in. "What?" I ask. "What is it?"

"We, uhh, we should wait for Jemmy," Mom says. She gives me a quick, intense look before refocusing her attention on her coffee.

Just then Jemmy comes bounding down the stairs with his tablet. "Hey guys!" he calls out, "You should see—there's these things called capybaras. They're like guinea pigs but *huge* and they live mostly in the water but also on land and they can run as fast as a horse!" He climbs up onto the stool between Dad and me and shows him the image on his tablet. "See!"

"Oh. Yeah," Dad says.

"Yeah, they can weigh sixty or even seventy kilos! See Mom?" He pushes his tablet along the countertop so both Mom and I can see the photo, and continues, "They're as big as Mutt! Wouldn't he be surprised if we came across one in the marsh!" He turns to me and says, "Maybe I could ride it and have a race with you and PeePee!" As he always does when he uses his nickname for my horse, he giggles. It's charming, someone waking up in a good mood like that.

"No, you couldn't race me and *Peony*, because for one thing, even if it weighed seventy kilos you'd be too big for it. You don't ride Mutt do you? And for two, there are no capybaras in our marsh." Although it would normally be a welcome distraction, I barely notice the four-syllable word.

"I *know*." He snorts and clicks his tongue, something he's recently begun doing when he has a *Duh!* moment, probably because Jimmy does it. He's also gotten adept at mansplaining, also like Jimmy, even though neither of them is technically a man.

"They live in South America," he continues, "but if there were..." his sentence drifts off with his thoughts as he scrolls through something else in his tablet. "Oh! And it's a good thing we don't have anacondas because they eat capybaras."

I look at Mom. She bites her lower lip, gets off the stool and goes to the far counter to make herself another cup of coffee. The Keurig gurgles and when it stops, she squares her shoulders, lifts her head, turns back to face us, and says, "Jemmy! Kids! Your dad and I have something important to talk to you about."

Jemmy's attention is still totally focused on his tablet. I take it out of his hands and slide it along the counter to my left where he can't reach it.

"Hey!" he squeals. He suddenly has half a dozen hands on multi-articulated arms grabbing after the tablet, almost enough to push me out of the way. You take his tablet from him at your peril.

"Mom?" I feel my frown. I can't say more.

She takes the tablet and sets it next to the sink and when Jemmy squawks again, Mom shushes him. He gives her a look then as if coming to the same conclusion I did, that he's going to have to listen, he relaxes.

"You guys," Mom says, "The first thing I want to say is that both Dad and I love you very much. Nothing will ever change that. But sometimes, some other things change."

Now my throat is tightening. I gulp a few times to try and rid myself of the lump.

"Something changed?" Jemmy asks.

"Your father...Dad...isn't going to live here anymore."

Jemmy looks puzzled, then asks, "He's not going to live here?" He turns and asks Dad, "Where are you going to live?"

"I have a place. Another house."

"But why? Did you want your own room?"

"It's just that...er...like your Mom said, things change..."

"Why don't you want to live here anymore? Will I ever see you again?"

"Yeah, buddy, of course you'll see me! We'll still see each other lots! I love you. I'm still going to be your Dad."

"Then why aren't you going to live here?"

"Your Daddy and I just can't live together anymore," Mom says.

"But...but I want him to stay here!" Jemmy cries out as looks at Mom; his voice rises an octave and he squirms on his stool, turning to face Dad again. "Daddy, I want you to stay here! I don't want you to live somewhere else!"

Dad pulls Jemmy into a hug as he starts to cry. All of us, Dad included, are teary-eyed now. Mom comes around the island and joins Dad in hugging Jemmy.

"Oh, sweetie," Mom says. She continues squeezing him tight, rubbing his back, and saying, "It'll be okay," over and over until Jemmy is able to calm himself. I start quietly sniffing, but when Jemmy looks at me, his face so small and wearing such an expression of anguish, I sob out loud.

After a minute or two, Jemmy collects himself a bit, and tells Dad, "I didn't mean to make you mad when I lost my salamander in your car. I forgot, that's all. I just forgot! I won't do it again!"

"It's nothing you did, buddy."

"Daddy isn't mad at you and he will always love you, sweetie. Your Dad and I are going to get a divorce, but there is no such thing as parent-child divorce. Parent love never dies." Mom releases him and fixes him with a look. "And your Dad and I will always take care of you. We're going to be fine. You're going to be fine. You'll see Daddy often and he'll still take you to karate or the pool, just like always. Okay?"

After a moment, tears streaming down his face, Jemmy nods and says, "Okay."

Mom kisses his forehead, then goes back around the island, picks up her mug, takes several deep breaths, and faces us again. "His new place has bedrooms for you. You can go and have sleepovers with him."

A hurricane of emotions nearly overcomes me. Jemmy thinks Dad left because of the Rotten Salamander Incident, which is ridiculous. Dad thinks Jemmy is cute and funny and a Perfect Boy, but I know I'm a disappointment. How many times has he told me a young lady must acquire finesse? I think back to all the make-up and hair tips he's offered over the years and his unfailing ability to spot dirty fingernails.

Then I give myself a mental headshake. This has nothing to do with me or Jemmy. For a while, I've had a feeling things weren't right between them. Does he have a girlfriend? Does Mom have a boyfriend?

Is that why she's been away so much? Maybe her overnights aren't job-related at all. Are we going to have to go and visit Dad and his new girlfriend? Will some stranger come to live with us?

I can't ask these questions now. I forget about making toast, and while they're both busy reassuring Jemmy, I take my mug of Cinnaswirl-infused coffee up to my room. As I'm going up the stairs, I hear Jemmy ask, "Is there a marsh at your new place?"

I don't hear the answer. I wish it was as simple for me as whether or not Dad's new place has a marsh, capybaras or no capybaras.

I SPEND SOME TIME ON my latest story while I finish my coffee, sticking my head out the door now and then to listen for voices. When it sounds like they've moved out of the kitchen, I go down. I see Jemmy on the patio and likely Mom is out there too, probably plucking dead flowers off her Rose of Sharon. No sign of Dad. I make it through the house without any of them seeing me.

While I'm doing barn chores, I mull over the situation and conclude it's Dad's fault things have wrong. It might not be something big, just a gradual accumulation of little things like never doing the grocery shopping or leaving his dirty dishes on the counter right above the dishwasher instead of putting them *in* the dishwasher, or never taking the empty bottles back, or always having the TV on when it would be nice to have some quiet. Mom probably got fed up, raising us kids basically alone as she's often told him she has to, because he's always so busy with his iPad or phone he might as well not even be there.

Maybe things won't be all that different with him living in his own place. Maybe they'll decide not to split up because then, as Jemmy says, Dad can have his own room, so they won't be nattering at each other all the time. Dad might realize he should put his phone or iPad down once in a while and promise to do better so she'll take him back.

From the barn door, I see Dad taking boxes out to his car. He gets in and drives off. I guess he'll be back for more before long. I hope it's when I'm not home.

I decide I need to tell Jimmy and Angie the news, but I don't want a bunch of drama and I'm not sure I can spit it all out without getting to that point, you know, where you can't talk you're so choked up. So I send texts.

Angie responds: "OMG that's too bad."

Jimmy responds: "On my way."

In twenty minutes, he cycles into the yard and right up to the barn. "Hey," I say.

He get off his bike, props it against the barn, and comes to me. His eyes look extra huge behind his thick lenses and he does something he's never done before: gives me a hug. I find myself hugging him back. It's a little awkward given our height differential, and also, he isn't a hugger probably owing to a hug-free childhood.

When he steps away from me, "I'm sorry, Lisa," is all he says.

I study his face, note how pinched it looks, and realize he feels bad too. Why shouldn't he? He never had a real home, just a father in jail and a drug-addicted abusive mother who dragged him from one bad place to another. Since he started hanging out here, he's become almost-family. He's probably wondering what it means for him, too.

"I'm sorry too," I tell him.

"I'd go with you to your lesson, but I think maybe Jemmy and your mom..."

"Yeah," I say, "they would love to see you."

FOCUSING ON WHAT WE'RE doing in the lesson not only keeps Peony's mind off the Gremlin Bush but it also keeps mine off the morning's bombshell. I'm not sad, exactly; just worried, wondering what other changes might be coming. Will we be able to keep the house? If we have to move to something smaller and less expensive in town, what will happen to Peony?

Dad will have to pay child support, but what if he doesn't? Mom has a good job. They both do. But I think they have a lot of bills because I've heard them arguing about it from time to time. How will they be able to afford two houses? Should I offer to pitch in my McDonald's pay?

I don't ask Mom for a ride to my afternoon shift at McDonald's because I'm not ready for twenty minutes of alone time with her. Somehow I stumble through my four-hour shift. My mind is elsewhere, and for once it's not because I'm in my make-believe world but in my actual world. I make a couple of blunders. Even the Old Manager gets snarky with me and takes me off the drive-through. I'm relegated to the burger line and she suggests I give a career change some thought, maybe yard work which would allow me to spend my time daydreaming without annoying customers by screwing up orders.

There's a lot going on inside my head: Mom and Dad splitting; Angie Missing in Action half the time and then the whole thing with her and Coop and now Jarrett; the Coven's new nickname for me; Jarrett being all weird; the hot new guy in the neighbourhood possibly snapped up by Nicole; still don't have my DL (Driver's License, if you didn't know) even though my eighteenth birthday is coming up and everyone my age has had theirs for years—all that, and here I am, back flipping burgers with even Old Manager mad at me. It's an all-around lousy way to start my Grade Twelve school year.

Angie Meets Jarrett

AS IT TURNS OUT, JARRETT does speak to me again, but not until Friday after school. I'm busy shoving books into my backpack when I get a text. It's Dwayne! Finally! He says he's on his way to Nanaimo and will see me tomorrow. I get this funny feeling in my chest that I imagine is what poets and romance writers mean when they talk about hearts skipping a beat.

Maybe it's not joy, but apprehension. I haven't seen him for so long I don't even know if we're still a couple. And you notice he doesn't say he's coming home, just that he's on his way? It could just be a visit. How to respond? I'm pondering this as I step through the door and out into the parking lot on my way to Angie's car. You know it's not hers, really, but as I mentioned, she has it so much it might as well be. So I just call it Angie's car.

I decide to text Dwayne back to let him know I have a lesson at Elke's in the morning and have to work in the afternoon. He should know he can't just show up back in town with hardly any notice and expect me to be available! If we're still an item, he should suggest going to Elke's with me. I'm not going to re-arrange my plans! The show is just a few weeks off so my lesson is important, and the McDonald's schedule is set at least a week in advance. I could call in sick, but I'm already on the Big Manager's shit list and Old Manager isn't all that thrilled with me either so I don't want to attract any more negative attention. I could see if they can get someone else but I don't want to give up four hours' pay! End result: I'm barely watching where I'm going and almost collide with Jarrett.

"Sorry," I mumble. Why did I apologize? He's not on his phone. You'd think he could have stayed out of my way. I take a step sideways and go to walk around him, but he turns and walks beside me.

"'S okay, my fault," he says. "I was hoping to catch you. Where ya goin'?"

"Home. Whereja think?" I say, and give him my best stink eye.

I know you're thinking, why is she rude when she's promised her friend she would invite him to come for a visit so she can introduce them and here's her chance? It's a valid point, but there are two reasons: one, I can't suddenly be all friendly and nice after he treated me so badly or he'll think he's Totally Awesome and a Smooth Talker and Irresistible; and two, I don't want to introduce Angie to him. I know how awful he can be, she doesn't need that in her life on top of everything else, and anyway, she's not here to see me talking to him.

Jarrett is undeterred. I told you my stink eye wasn't all that good. He says, "Me too. Wanna ride?"

"I have a ride." We're in front of Angie's car already. Why couldn't she have arrived at school late this morning so she'd have to park in the overflow lot or down the street somewhere? I guess that only happens when it's raining and you don't have a jacket. I think maybe I'll walk past pretending I don't see her, but she gives the horn a short toot and there goes that idea. I see her teeth so I know she's happy and she's already opening her door.

She slides out and says, "Hi!"

"Um, hi. Sorry I'm late."

"No problem, I just got here." She closes the door and comes to stand next to me. If there was dog shit in her path she would've stepped right in it because I doubt she's seeing any-thing but Jarrett. I stand there speechless wondering how to avoid the inevitable. She roots me with her elbow and says, "Lisa! Introduce us!"

I still haven't learned to stay out of range of those elbows. "Er, Angie, this is Jarrett."

She sticks out her hand; he takes it, and they both say, "Pleased to meet you," in sync like a couple of trained parrots.

"Hey, guys," Jarrett says, "a bunch of us are going over to the skate bowl. Wanna go hang out?"

"Sure!" Angie says before I can even blink.

"Great! My car?"

"Um, no, I don't wanna come back here to get my car after. We'll follow you," Angie says.

"Okay! See you over there!" He grins and clicks his tongue as he points a pretend gun hand at us, then turns and walks away with a bounce in his step.

I'm thinking, what the hell was that? But Angie is all squirmy and giddy and giggly like she has kittens in her shirt. I step away in case she's going to do that elbow thing again but she's already getting back into her car. She slams the door and buckles her seatbelt before powering the window down and calling out, "Come on! Let's get going!"

"The skate bowl? To watch a bunch of farting, swearing, vaping, smoking guys show off?"

"Oh, Lisa, you're so judgmental!"

"Comes with being a Libra," I say.

Angie frowns. I know she wants to say that's no excuse because she's told me it isn't about a hundred times and when she calls me Lisa Libra it's not a compliment as I've mentioned, but her thoughts have raced on.

"If Jarrett's going other hot guys will be there too, like the guys on his basketball team. I don't think they all fart and smoke!"

"They don't all smoke, anyway." Sure, I'm generalizing and there's bound to be nice guys there too, but I don't want to be one of the girls hanging around providing an audience. They do pretty cool stuff and I guess it's entertaining for half an hour or so, but the few times I've been to the skate park are more than enough. I'd a thousand times rather get home in time to ride Peony and there's barn chores besides.

I'm surprised Angie is so anxious to go when just minutes before she wanted to come and help groom Peony who she's loved from the first day we saw her at the rescue. Surely she realizes how pathetic we'd look if we showed up because one afternoon Jarrett was nice for a few minutes? After The Coop Debacle you'd think she'd know better. I tell her, "Have you never heard of playing hard to get? Besides, I don't trust him"

"You said that before and I still think you're wrong."

"You've forgotten what an asshole he was last year? And now he's nice? A one-eighty for no apparent reason?"

"There is a reason! He's sorry, that's the reason."

"Well, I'm not going to run after him. But you go if you want."

"Come on, Lisa."

"Um, no. You go ahead."

Angie doesn't coax; she's so anxious to leave that as soon as I step away she pulls out of the parking stall, wearing a big smile and giving me a wave as she goes.

"Jeez, if I didn't get my feet outta the way she'd've run over them." Couldn't she have at least offered to drop me off at home first? I guess it's just too far out of her way.

A couple of kids on the sidewalk give me an odd look as if they think I might be having an episode, standing in the parking lot muttering to myself. I smile and acknowledge them with a lift of my chin, then take a couple of deep breaths, shrug my backpack into a more comfortable position and head for the sidewalk. With luck, I haven't missed the bus. As I round the corner of the school, I see it pulling away. So now I have an hour's walk home.

What happened to the Angie who just wanted to stay home? What about the Coop Debacle? And she leaves me to walk home because she's in such a panic to get with Jarrett?

I head for the Parkway Trail, wondering why I can't keep friends. I know what you're thinking, Angie hasn't dropped me and maybe I'm over-reacting. Maybe Jarrett is genuinely contrite. Maybe Angie will settle down after he either does or doesn't become her boyfriend. Or maybe I'm just doomed to be a loner all my life.

Oh! If you're wondering about Peony and me and if we've made any progress this week, I'm still not getting a nice steady contact on the outside rein and the inside rein? Forget about it. I'm never sure what diagonal I'm on and left lead? Forget about that, too. It seems hopeless.

Maybe I should save Mom the cost of the lessons and go back to plunking around the trails in my old western saddle. Alone.

Maybe I should give up.

Against the World

I KNOW, THAT WAS A pathetic bunch of Poor Me Thoughts I had on my way home Friday. I felt a lot better after spending some time with NeeNee and when Bailey dropped in on her way home from Elke's, I was super glad I didn't miss her.

My barn is nowhere near as tricked-out as Elke's, which has a tack room with a couple of loveseats and even a biffy with a shower, but Bailey said it was cute and was in no hurry to leave. We hung out. Bailey helped me groom and so on. She mentioned NeeNee's mane was going to take a lot of work to get braided for the show because it's long, and thanks to her draft parent, very thick. She showed me how to get started pulling and shortening it.

I know what you're thinking, we pulled NeeNee's mane? Yup. It's not like hair pulling when kids fight which hurts although the hair usually doesn't come right out, but we did pull NeeNee's hair right out. It's not as bad as it sounds because horses don't have the nerve endings we do and we didn't pull out very much. Bailey said I should pull a bit every time I groom her, especially after riding when she's warm because the hair comes out more easily when her pores are open. If I do a little every day, once I get it to a manageable thickness it will be easy to keep that way. She is going to bring her electric clippers with her tonight to shorten it nicely without leaving a hard straight line, and then she'll show me how to braid so I can do some practice braids before I have to braid her whole mane for the show.

I really wish I had started lessons at Elke's a long time ago so I could have had Bailey as a friend sooner. It's true I took a few lessons when my old horse, Wembly, was sound enough but that was about three summers ago and Marci/Bailey weren't boarding their horses there then.

Altogether it was a pleasant enough week-end even though Angie was too busy with Jarrett to hang out with me. My lesson was good and the run-through for the show went so well I'm starting to feel more confident about it. I got to work five minutes early and didn't do anything to make Big Manager's hemorrhoids flare up. Mom and Jemmy really didn't seem any different than usual. Except for no lawnmowing going on, Dad not being home wasn't much different than Dad being home. If this is the new normal, it's okay.

Monday morning, I start toward Angie's locker. I'm anxious to know how it went with Jarrett. I texted her a couple times but her only response was OMG!!! and the happy face emoji. Which doesn't tell you much.

You might be thinking I hope she's at least a little sorry for dropping me like a hot potato and running off with Jarrett, and High Five to you! Of course, if she hit it off with Jarrett and he really is back to being the nice guy he was pre-Laurie Ann, I will be happy for her. But as you know, I don't trust him, his sudden change that is, and with her mother sick she has enough stress in her life and doesn't need more.

As I round the corner, I see Angie's there all right, and Jarrett is with her. I stop dead in my tracks when she loops an arm around his waist and snuggles in for a body-pressing hug, and then they kiss! I can't believe things have progressed to a public display like that so quickly! When they finally break it up, they turn and start toward me.

"Hey," Jarret says, "hi, Lisa!"

"Hey," I say. By now they have reached where I'm standing as if my boots are nailed to the floor.

"You jammed out on Friday," he says.

"Brilliant observation," I respond.

They both frown at me but Jarrett asks, "Why didn't you come?"

"I had too much to do."

"She doesn't really have anything else to do, she's just a stick in the mud," Angie says as she sidles close to him and takes his arm. "We had a nice time, Lisa. We went to the food court after."

She's looking at Jarrett as if he's the Sun and the Moon, and I guess I should make some comment. "Nice!" is all I can come up with. I know I should be happier for my friend, and I would be if I didn't think he had some devious motive.

"Well, see you at lunch," I say, then spin and practically sprint to get away from them, back to my locker to get my books for the morning's classes.

Of course, I don't see her at lunch. I imagine she went somewhere with Jarrett. So it's just me and Jimmy.

"I don't think Angie will be joining us," I tell him. "It's like she's gone bonkers over Jarrett, even though they only officially met on Friday."

"I know," Jimmy says, "I saw them on my way here. They were in that herd of basketball players at the display cases in the foyer and then the whole mob headed for the door. She looked right at me but I don't think she even saw me."

"Well, Jimmy, I guess it's you and me against the world." I pull my all-time most favourite sandwich, tuna and lettuce on sourdough, out of my lunch bag, unwrap it and take a bite. I realize Jimmy doesn't seem to have anything but a granola bar for lunch. Last year he almost never had a lunch at all, but since he's been a ward of the state he is seldom sandwichless. "Hey! You eat your lunch between periods or something?"

"Naw, I just..." he sighs.

"You just what? Forgot to buy food?"

"Well, you know I mostly eat at work. Haven't looked at my bread for a couple days, thought it was still good, but it was moldy. You should see it! It's like a science project, the whole bag is filled with filaments of bread mold. It created its own terrarium. It doesn't smell too bad if I keep the bag shut so I'm leaving it to see how far it goes..."

"James Rice, I don't believe you! That had to take longer than a couple of days. And it's going to be spewing out mold spores that will get on everything and you'll have moldy...umm...everything!"

He shrugs and pulls a notebook out of his backpack, opening it on the table in front of him. Apparently, if Moldy Everything is the price to be paid for a Moldy Bread Experiment, he's willing to pay it.

I push the unmangled half of my sandwich to him. "Eat this. You can pay me for it by going over my biology assignment for this afternoon."

He accepts the sandwich without argument. I make a mental note to tell Mom he may not be doing all that well, taking care of himself. When he became a ward of the state, he went into foster care if you can call it care. There is such a shortage of foster homes, old kids like him are sometimes housed in hotel rooms and a social worker shows up once in a while. This is why he's living at the Northgate.

You don't need to pity him, though, at least not for living in a hotel room. He's happy about it because living with his mother was Hell On Earth. She shows up to visit him once in a while but it usually ends with her asking for money so it's not a good thing or an indication they might reconcile.

He doesn't want to go back to live with her, that's for sure. He's always mentioning how nice it is to have hot water in the shower. So he showers a lot, but he's often short on groceries. This is not for lack of money, it's just that he's too busy thinking. He needs someone to take care of him even though he's so brainy; you know, someone to remind him to get groceries and so on.

I remember hearing Einstein was famous for forgetting to do up his fly. I don't think Jimmy's that bad, but you get the idea. And he must get lonely, too. There are other foster kids in the hotel but he's just too different to fit in with them. In fact, he has a hard time fitting in anywhere because he's such a Serious Little Brainiac. (His mother used to refer to him as That Snotty Little Know-It-All. That's not nice, but Serious Little Brainiac is okay, isn't it?)

You remember I mentioned he's a grade behind me but has Grade Twelve courses: Chemistry and Biology, the latter likely no surprise to you after the Snake Hibernaculum Discussion. Anyway, after we've consumed my lunch, we go to my locker for my biology notebook, then find seats in the study hall and he reads through the assignment. We get into a discussion about endoplasmic reticulum, I make a couple of changes to my answers, and before you know it lunch hour is over and it's back to class.

YOU PROBABLY GATHERED I hadn't seen Angie over the week-end, and now I've barely seen her all week, at least in the way of hanging out like we used to, because she's always doing something with Jarrett. Before The Coop Debacle I wouldn't have believed it if you told me she'd be that kind of friend.

Now I'm shocked at something else: she's given up her Tasteful Private School Look in favour of Floozy. It happened overnight. Well, *overweek* would be more accurate.

One day she was in leggings and a tunic top much like everyone and the next day, jeans so low-rise I could see half her lacey thong as she walked ahead of me. By Wednesday, some kind of T-shirt you could see through in places and it was very obvious she wasn't wearing a bra. Thursday, she did wear a bra, which was frequently visible because her shirt ended just under her boobs. She paired this with the low-rise jeans so it's quite a picture both coming and going, and definitely *going* when she's hunched over putting stuff in her backpack. Friday, don't ask. She must have been doing a lot of shopping, because except for the leggings, these are clothes I've never seen before.

She still wears leggings, of course; everyone does, well not the boys except a couple of guys who sometimes wear something like leggings under baggy shorts, but you knew that. Now she wears them with crop tops, leaving little to the imagination. I wonder what those super strict parents of hers think! It makes me sad to see such a change for the worse and I still can't believe how fast it happened. Just one week with Jarrett and she looks like she'd fit in with The Coven? She does look happy, though, and I guess that's the important thing.

I know a few other girls well enough to join them for lunch and there's always Jimmy. Besides my little brother, I might be Jimmy's only friend, although he has joined the chess club so for him, there's the promise of more friends on the horizon.

I always include Jimmy and the other girls I mentioned think he's okay, too. He's generous with his time, helping everyone with their school work, so that makes him a Good Guy To Know. Also, I think he grew about six inches over summer and he's got more than one shirt since his clothing allowance doesn't go to pay for his mother's meth so coupled with the frequent showers, he doesn't look grubby and out of place like he did last year. What seems like a lifetime ago, Angie and I gave him a T-shirt that read "Grade A Rice". It was to make him feel better when he was in the hospital. His last name is Rice. Get it?

I wanted to add "Short Grain" which is a nickname I gave him, you know, like " Grade A Short Grain Rice", but Angie nixed that. It's not like I called him that to his face. Still, Angie was afraid it might slip out and it would make him feel bad for being small which is something he has no control over after all. He still favours T-shirts with clever phrases on them, such as "YOU MATTER, unless you multiply yourself by the speed of light squared, then YOU ENERGY", and so on. Don't ask me what it means. I suspect only geeks get it.

If you're thinking I'm suddenly popular or this group I'm mentioning is Top Tier, forget about it! I'm not and we're not. Daryl-Lyn and Sandy are just as ordinary-looking as I am; Julie would be attractive but for her huge glasses and her thinning hair (she has alopecia), and Connie is overweight. Very overweight. Members of The Coven bark like dogs when we walk by. For Connie, they make piggy sounds. You'd think those witches would realize everyone has feelings, wouldn't you? But you get my point. We're the Untouchables of Westview Secondary. Angie has escaped, which is next to impossible for an Untouchable. I guess should be happy for her.

I've spent every day after school riding and hanging out at Elke's or with Bailey either at my place or hers, so it's filled the Angie void. If you think I'm at Elke's so much because I'm taking a ton of lessons, forget about it, they're fifty bucks each! I'm thankful Mom pays for my one lesson a week and so far hasn't mentioned cutting out that expense. Fingers crossed. Elke lets me ride in her ring any time for free so long as I don't tell the others who don't board their horses there, as they have to pay. You can learn a lot watching other people's lessons and besides that, Bailey is helping me learn the Training Level tests I'll be riding at the show.

Bailey is going to call my tests for me so I don't forget where I'm going and end up off course. She says this is only because I'm just starting out and that I not only have to learn where all the letters are, but also memorize the tests so I can ride without a caller in future. So far all I know for sure is where X is (if you don't know, it's right in the middle of the arena and unlike the rest of the letters which are posted around the fence, there is no actual mark). This is where you stop and salute the judge before beginning the test and also where the test ends and you salute again.

Peony and I have been working hard on getting a nice square halt at X, which means her back feet are together and her front feet are together. Well, not together, together, just front feet beside each other and back feet beside each other, not one further back or in the case of the back feet, one sticking out the side. It's something you get points for and is more difficult than I expected. If it seems silly to focus on such a little thing, keep in mind the test is a series of Little Things that add up to a Big Thing. When you think about it, it's a lot like Life.

I still don't have my own dressage saddle although my bank account is growing. It goes kind of slow when your paycheque is less than a hundred and fifty dollars a month and my parents have never spoiled me by giving me a big allowance. I'm grateful for that as you can imagine.

I tried a saddle the Mane Street Tack Shop had in on consignment but it was too small and Marci says I might have to bite the bullet and order one to get a draft size and I didn't have enough for the used one at Mane Street even if it did fit, so there you go.

Don't get me wrong, I'm not in the market for a three thousand dollar saddle. The nice lady at Mane Street showed me a catalogue with "vegan saddles" which is a trendy way of saying they're made of fake leather. They cost between five and seven hundred dollars, and she would be happy to order one for me. They come with an adjustable part and she gave me a measuring device so I know for sure there's a size that would fit Peony. So I'm setting my sights on the five hundred dollar model. I think I'll have enough money by January, if I get money as birthday and Christmas gifts. In the meantime, I have downloaded pictures from the internet and put them up in various inconspicuous places such as the front of the fridge, the door to the garage, and all the bathroom mirrors. I told Mom it's just to keep my goal front of mind. Even so, she said no one else needs my goal front of mind, and took them all down.

If you think I'm so anxious to get my own saddle because Marci has been nattering at me to give her saddle back, you can forget about it. She says she's totally fine with me using hers as she doesn't need it anyway. Of course if she doesn't need it she could sell it, but she can't do that as long as I have it. She hasn't mentioned that. That's how nice she is.

Mom went with Bailey and me when we went to Mane Street Tack and Feed and she bought me a new black dressage bridle. I am totally stoked! It has shiny patent leather piping and a row of crystals on the browband. I picked up a couple of other things in the consignment section: white breeches with only a few black stains in the crotch which Bailey says are from the dye in the saddle and all her breeches have them, and a black jacket. Of course the breeches are too short. When your legs are as long as mine, that's inevitable. They'll be inside my boots anyway so no one will notice.

I bought a new pair of English boots, not the hundreds of dollars ones, the fifty dollar rubber ones. But really, couldn't one pair of the used leather boots have fit me? They're about the price of the rubber ones and wouldn't make my feet sweat. On the day I wore my new boots without socks I almost couldn't get them off again. I thought I'd have to cut them off and there goes fifty bucks out the window, and I'd be English bootless besides! Luckily, a few hours later my feet had cooled down I guess, because I finally got them off. Anyway. Despite the rubber boots and short breeches, with a white blouse I look fine, in my opinion.

Oh, and I posted a photo of Peony wearing her beautiful new dressage bridle on Facebook and got seven Likes! This proves I have a lot of aunts and cousins. Well, there was one person who said, "Fuck that's a big head shoulda named him T-Rex". I don't even know the person who posted that and it's no one on my (very short) friends list. Must be a Friend of a Friend. You have to keep in mind Facebook Friends are not the same as Friends. I replied with the Angry Face Emoji and put it out of my mind.

If you're thinking there's a lot to do to get organized for a horse show and that it sure seems to run into money, High Five to you! Elke says a horse hobby is not for the financially squeamish. If being financially squeamish means broke, that's me. Even getting all that second-hand stuff, my dressage saddle account has been decimated.

Still, I'm elated and apprehensive and giddy about the show, which is less than a month away.

Okay now I know you're thinking, what is all this drivel about Angie and Jarrett and Jimmy and Daryl-Lyn and Sandy and Julie and the dressage bridle and Facebook and Bailey reading the tests and so on, and nothing about what happened when Dwayne came?

Remember, you asked for this.

Dylan

DYLAN COMES OUT OF the medical center and hurries along the concourse out into the bright sunlight, heading for the chutes. His wrist feels better now that it's taped up tight and he's checked to make sure he can get his glove on over it. He's got his rigging. He's good to go.

The bull riding is about to start. He's pretty far down the order of go, but it's customary for riders to help at the chutes, maybe standing on the rails ready to grab a rider to stop them falling under the bull should it freak out in the chute, or to assist with putting the rigging on the bull.

He gets to the chute area and finds he's not needed on the rails, so he focuses on getting his rope brushed and rosined. He's psyching himself up for the ride ahead, trying to force his friend's warning out of his mind. Still, it keeps coming back: *Don't let his name fool you that bull ain't no one's friend! Them Mexican fighting bulls is bad news and that one has never been rode, not even by better cowboys than you. You'll be lucky if he don't kill you.*

Dylan laughed and said, *I was born lucky.* Bold words. Reckless words. A grin to hide the fact his guts were in knots.

The bull he drew, My Friend Fred, is known to be mean. As soon as the gate opens, he usually rears and tries to clean the rider off on the corner post of the chute. He has crippled cowboys with that move! The frightened look in his girlfriend's eyes, her reluctance to let go of his hand when they parted, preys on his mind as well.

Then Fred is run into the chute, bellowing in rage, wringing his tail. He sprays feces as he goes and the stench assaults Dylan's nose. The chute boss tells him he's up; he tries to concentrate on the details of getting ready to ride but it goes by in a blur, his friend's warning is on a continuous loop in his brain. *You'll be lucky if he don't kill you...if he don't kill you...kill you...*

He takes a few deep breaths, gulps, squares his shoulders, then climbs over the rails and carefully settles onto the bull, feeling the heat of the animal's body radiating through his jeans, smelling the fresh manure. It's a comfort to note two big cowboys are on the rails along with the flanker, hovering over him.

Fred bellows and tries to climb out the front of the chute. Dylan's foot slips off the rails but the cowboys grab him and easily have him up and out of harm's way.

The bull quiets and Dylan settles on him again. Fred bobs around a little but he's quit bellowing and now just snorts and flings his head around. Dylan quickly rubs his rope to warm the rosin and make it good and sticky. He lays the rope over his hand and with his left fist, pounds his fingers down. He leans back and takes several deep breaths. His feet are up on the bull's shoulders where he wants them, so he nods.

The gate swings open. My Friend Fred leaps into action. Dylan jabs his spurs hard into the bull's shoulders in hopes it stops him from rearing and makes him lunge out of the chute instead. Great! It worked! Then he's riding a leaping, kicking, whirling tornado and his unconscious mind takes over.

He's about to be launched when he hears the horn. Fred throws in a leaping twist and Dylan is bucked off into the middle of the spinning whirlwind. He can't get loose. Another jump and he manages to free his hand but not before the bull swings his head around, hooks him with a horn, and throws him over his back. He lands flat. Scrambles to his feet. Fred charges and smashes into his chest. His breath is knocked out of him with a *whoosh!* and he's thrown to the ground. Before the *OHHH!*

from the crowd has faded and before the bull can grind him into the dirt, the bullfighters in their sneakers and shorts and cowboy hats are all around him, drawing him off.

A mounted cowboy gets a rope around Fred's horns and his little Quarter Horse pulls him a few steps away before Fred bellows and lunges at him. He charges the horse for only a heartbeat then spins away, looking for something that can't move as fast, and sets his sights on Dylan, who's still on all fours. When he charges back toward Dylan, the pick-up rider loses the lasso. Dylan tries to scramble the last few feet to the fence but the bull is too fast and lifts him on his horns, tossing him into the air like a rag with a knot tied in it.

Now he's on the ground looking skyward. He tries to get up but can't make his legs move. He turns his head, looking for the bull, and sees him just a couple of meters away. Snorting. Pawing. The bullfighters are all around him, even running right in front of him and punching his nose, but the bull isn't distracted and charges again.

As the huge head and hooves come at him, Dylan has a split second to think, *I rode him, but my luck sure ran out today.*

IF YOU FIGURED OUT Dylan is really Dwayne, High Five to you! I told you it's a bad idea to screw over a writer because you might get killed off in their next story!

I would like to point out that at least he rode that bull to the horn, the first cowboy to do so, so he would be a legend although I imagine that would be small comfort to someone who's dead.

Of course Dwayne didn't really die under a bull's hooves in a rodeo arena, although he says he got interested in rodeo this summer and wants to try bull riding, but he's dead to me all the same.

To his credit, he was nice about dumping me, spouting the tired clichés found in every True Confessions story: it's not you, it's me; we can still be friends, and so on. In fact, he's staying in Alberta so the promise to remain friends is a hollow one or at least easy to keep since he'll be a thousand kilometers away. He says he loves the work on the ranch, the country is beautiful, and so on. I wonder if he'll still think so after a couple of months of prairie winter.

    He says the people are nice, too. He admitted there was one nice person in particular. She's the daughter of the ranch owner, another True Confessions cliché if there ever was one. She has a truck and a horse trailer because she's a barrel racer. I'm guessing she doesn't have freckles or legs that are ridiculously long so her pants are always the right length. I bet she's a better kisser than I am, too, even though as you know, I had quite a bit of practice with Jarrett a few years ago and I won't deny Dwayne and I went at it as often as possible before he left for Alberta. She may even be nice, I guess.

    I thought about killing her off in the story too, but didn't, for two reasons: one, I couldn't figure out a way that she would reasonably be in the arena to get stomped by the bull. Would she run in to give the dying Dylan comfort? That would be nonsensical, she wouldn't have time, and the other cowboys would stop her for sure. And two, she doesn't know me, it's not like Dwayne and I were married, and he's hot so I can't blame her for going after him. I guess that's more than two reasons, but it gets tiring putting in a bunch of semi-colons and not the best idea since *The Industry Canada Style Guide for Writers and Editors* says you should use them sparingly.

    Oh, and since we're talking about stories, you might be wondering about *Nikki and Jackson* and what Mrs. Wiebe thought of that story, being as it was the last one of the course. Have you given it your own rating so you could compare it to Mrs. Wiebe's score? Like anywhere from an F to an A plus? If you did, it was a waste of time because Mrs. Wiebe doesn't give percentage marks, she just goes through and uses purple ink to mark stuff she likes or to write nice comments. For corrections and other stuff she doesn't like, she uses the standard red ink. This shows she has the eye of an artist because purple and red go together well, in my opinion.

I'm happy to say there wasn't a lot of red ink, but neither was there much purple. That part was disappointing. I think she was somewhat put off by the subject matter. On the last page which was half blank so there was plenty of room to write, she noted the improvement in my use of comma splices (purple ink!) and said I should keep writing and start submitting stories everywhere I can. She listed some websites to get me started. Encouraging, right?

It would have been a whole lot more encouraging, though, if she hadn't gone on to say that if she didn't know me better, she might be concerned as the story is awfully dark. But she said she knows I have a huge respect and admiration for Stephen King, thinks I wrote the story in his style, and so she didn't feel a need to report me to the Mental Health Police. She ended that sentence with "LOL!" Maybe I should have Laughed Out Loud too. I would have, except I didn't see the humor in it.

So, no gold star. But then, she doesn't give out stars, gold or otherwise.

Trent

IT'S OFFICIAL, TRENT and Nicole are an item. I've seen them drive past about half a dozen times now. I guess Trent goes to a different school or maybe he's not still in school, because when I see Nicole around she's not with a guy. So I don't see them holding hands or smooching or anything, just in the car together. I figure if they don't see each other at school she has some other way of connecting with him like she has his phone number, ergo, boyfriend/girlfriend. So the Potential Boyfriend Pool has officially been drained. As you know, it was more of a puddle than a pool to start with. Maybe even just a slightly wet patch.

I'm considering killing Trent off in another story, but decide it's too harsh since he hasn't done anything to me, but you know, just to get him out of the Boyfriend Slightly Wet Patch in my mind. I decide to send him somewhere. That way if he comes to his senses and splits with Nicole, he can always come back and then of course he'd be boyfriend material again. Maybe he should get kidnapped by a press gang and made to work on a tall ship sailing around the world. He could be seen climbing fearlessly up the rigging to the crow's nest and shouting, "Land ho!" and so on.

Or possibly, he becomes an explorer and wants to go—where? Hasn't everything already been discovered? Outer space, I guess.

Or he could turn into a werewolf. From what I know of werewolves, it's an incurable affliction. In the unlikely event he were to ditch Nicole in favour of me, having to lock him up at those times of the month would be a Pain In The Patootie. Scratch that idea.

I should explain why it's unlikely Trent, or any guy for that matter, would prefer me over Nicole. She's little and cute while I'm big and not cute. She has big boobs and cute little feet. It's a wonder she doesn't tip over, she's so top-heavy. My size eleven shoes can easily be confused with Dad's and therefore, with any other guy's shoes. Well, not Dad's dress shoes, but you know, the other ones, especially since brightly-coloured running shoes have become so trendy. He even has a pink pair he wears with his pink polo shirt! Mom's feet are only half a size smaller than mine so it must have been a problem for her as well. It's kind of a relief, to me anyway, that Dad's shoes aren't in the mud room anymore so no confusion can arise. And boobs? I barely need a bra. I take after my mother in that department, too. Otherwise Mom and I don't look alike and she's shorter than me which has often prompted Dad to wonder where I get my height from and when I'm going to stop growing. (FYI I think I have.) The good thing about this is that with my big feet and no boobs, I am never in danger of tipping over.

Anyway. Because Nicole is small, she wears small clothes. (Duh!) About a year ago when we were still friends we shopped together. She has available to her every style of jeans and pants in the store plus there is a whole big section of Petites both at The Bay and all the clothing stores. Meanwhile, I'm stuck with a selection of three or four styles, all plain and boring, off the Tall Rack at Reitman's, and still have to check to make sure they have a big enough hem to let down to get the extra inch or two I need. Even at Mane Street where they have all kinds of awesome jeans, there are only a few with a thirty-six inch inseam and they're not the fancy ones.

I know what you're thinking: lots of people wear pants that end centimeters above the ankle and look great. You'd think I'd be all over that, but I'm not, possibly because of having to wear pants that were too short most of my life. When I wear them, I just look like I outgrew them. Plus I find my ankles get cold and even I am not enough of a dork to wear them with knee highs.

I should stipulate here that if I were to wear above-the-ankle pants with knee highs, I would look dorky but if you are rocking knee highs with above-the-ankle pants, likely it's not dorky when you do it, and High Five to you. Keep in mind I am no one's go-to person for fashion advice.

Nicole also has naturally blonde hair. You might wonder, as I do, why she persists in dying it various colours. She has the peaches and cream complexion of her English mother and gets zits so seldom it's not worth mentioning.

My hair is a mousy red-brown. I have dyed it a few times but it's time consuming and messy. The last time I tried dying my hair, you should've heard how Mom went on and on about ruining her best towels, as if we don't have a linen closet full of them! Anyway, I don't pay enough attention to keep on top of it, so dye jobs are so few and far between I end up with inches of regrowth. So, I have brassy red hair with inches of mousy red-brown regrowth. I have freckles and get zits on my forehead. You can see why Trent wouldn't trade Nicole for me.

You are probably thinking, why is she whining about her hair when all she has to do is pay more attention to it? You're right of course. But when you're already too tall, have big feet and small boobs, perfect hair dye jobs won't make a difference so it's not worth the trouble, in my opinion.

These thoughts are wandering through my mind as I ride Peony along the path next to the pavement, en route to Elke's. I barely notice we're in front of Trent's place, that's how far along I am in moving him out of contention as a boyfriend. Peony gives a little snort and jiggle and brings me back to earth. If you thought maybe she was surprised by a person standing near the road next to a Scary Bush, High Five to you! I'm surprised too. It's Trent. I recognize him by his lumpy bike riding clothing rather than his face because as I mentioned, I've never seen him without his helmet before. You're probably thinking, *another clue would be that this is right in front of where he lives, genius!* High Five to you, smarty pants.

He's standing with his hands on his hips, favouring one foot, and smiling. At me! As soon as we're near, he says, "Hi." A warm feeling floods me, he's that pretty, in a masculine way of course.

"Hi," I manage to respond, and feel my face getting red because that came out in a kind of squeak.

"I bet you're Jemmy's big sister," he says, and comes to stand on the road. I rein Peony in. He walks right up to Peony on her good-eye side and strokes her shoulder. I guess he's not afraid of horses after all. This is a reminder: you should never make assumptions.

He's standing so close I can almost feel the body heat radiating off him. I swallow (read: gulp) a couple of times to get my voice to return to normal and say, "Yeah." It comes out okay. I hope he means big in the sense of older and not like, frig, are you ever big! Of course he has no way of knowing how tall I am since I'm on NeeNee, but I notice if you were to put a ruler across from his head to NeeNee's withers, it would be higher on his end. This means he's taller than I am, always nice in a boyfriend.

Of course, it's more about the shoes. Maybe you think I'm making too much about the feet thing but consider this: if your feet are as big as your boyfriend's, it could be a problem getting your shoes mixed up if you should ever go someplace where you take your shoes off, such as a friend's house or some other situation I'll leave to your imagination. Think of how embarrassing it would be if he went to put his shoes back on only to discover you were already wearing them!

I should mention in case you aren't aware, ladies size eleven is smaller than a man's size eleven so I am only hoping for man's size ten and up, in a boyfriend.

I look down at his feet but it's hard to tell how big they are from here. It's amazing how thoughts like these can speed through a person's mind.

"My name's Trent."

"Umm, I'm, er, Lee...*Lisa*." Awkward! I stutter on my name?

Trent doesn't seem to notice, though. He's probably used to girls getting all tongue-tied in his presence. He just goes smoothly on with, "Pleased to meet you, Lisa. Jemmy said you had a horse. He's beautiful!"

"She's a she, but umm, thanks."

"Sorry, *she's* beautiful." He stands away again, hands on hips, and says, "Man, she's really big. You really have to have guts to ride such a huge animal!"

Guts? Not me. I've been riding since I was nine, and I know she's about as safe as a horse could be. "No, she's very safe," I tell him, "but I'd *never* have the guts to speed around on a motorbike like you do!" (Much better, right?)

"I don't think about it. I've been riding since I was about seven. It's what you're used to, I guess. Hey, Jemmy hasn't been around lately. Is he all right?"

"Yeah, he's fine. It's just that he's not very interested in motorized things. He likes creepy crawly slithery things. He made one hibernaculum and now he's making them all over." (Another chance to use that word!)

"He made a what?" he asks. His hair is mostly brown with a blonde streak, kind of long especially on top, and falls forward, covering one eye. I try not to stare but notice his nose is on the large side, with a bump at the bridge like he might have broken it at one time. Call me crazy but I think it's attractive. But the best thing about his face? Big, bright, sparkling blue eyes.

"Hibernaculum. It's something snakes like. It's to attract them, a safe place for them to hibernate."

"Oh. So, how do you make one?"

"Near as I can tell, it's just a pile of wood. He got instructions off the internet."

"Cool! He's a smart kid."

Smart? Jemmy? I guess he is. "It comes with a price. I never know what he might have in his grubby little mitts that he needs to show me."

Trent chuckles, shuffles his feet a little, and smooths his forelock back. "I see you going by all the time, figure you must be on your way to that big farm at the end of the road. Am I right?"

"Yup. Elke, the owner, is my coach. We're getting ready for a show in a few weeks."

"Oh yeah? Like, jumping?"

"No. Dressage."

"Dressage? What's that?"

"At my level? Just a bunch of circles."

"Circles?"

"Really nice circles!" I laugh, and snort loudly. What a complete idiot! But he's just smiling at me, so I rush on. "My friend's boyfriend says watching dressage is like watching paint dry, if that helps."

"Oh. He's not a fan of horses? I've never been around horses but I do like them, or at least appreciate them. I was wondering if I could go with you, maybe see what that horse farm is all about, sometime?"

"Sure. Okay." I feel heat rising in my face. Should I suggest he come with me now? I want to be cool. I need to act like I'm too busy or have too many demands on my time or I'm on my way to something so important it can't possibly be right now. "How about now?" I hear myself say. Okay, it was out before I had a chance to think any more about it.

"Can't right now, Lisa," he says.

So why did I open my big mouth? I look like I have nothing much going on and he's on his way to something so important it can't possibly be right now. I feel stupid and to make matters worse, I'm sure I'm turning red.

But he continues, "I'm on my way to meet my buddies at The Wastelands. There's a big Motocross this weekend and we're practicing. But maybe tomorrow?"

Oh! Not so bad then! I give a *who cares* kind of shrug and say, "If you want."

"Can I call you?"

"Er, sure." Now my face is so hot it must be glowing. I fuss with Peony's reins so she jiggles about a little, as a distraction.

He pulls his phone out of his pocket and in a moment, says, "Okay. Lisa what?"

"Rogney. R-O-G-N-E-Y."

He enters it, asks for my number and I give him that. When he's done, he says, "Great! I'll text you tomorrow!" He turns and scurries back to the path that leads to his driveway, half turning once to give me a wave and a smile before disappearing behind the bushes.

I take a deep breath, tell that thumping in my chest to knock it off, then continue on my way. When I hear a vehicle I turn in the saddle to see a truck with a motorbike in the box leaving Trent's driveway.

Now what? I tell myself: settle down, he's probably curious about Elke's place, it's not a date, he just wanted to ask about Jemmy, he's with Nicole isn't he? And so on. But the warmth flooding my insides won't subside. If I was on the ground, I'd probably jump around, which would make me look like I was having an episode, not that anyone's watching. Maybe some up-down-up-down-up-down action will make it stop. I push NeeNee into a trot. Problem: I don't know which diagonal to rise on, since we're going in a straight line.

I make it to Elke's without figuring it out. Bailey is already trotting around the ring. I don't need to mention she's on her horse, do I? One of the young students that's always hanging around is at the gate. I smile at her but inside I'm thinking she has probably known her diagonals for a year, damn her, even though she's barely a teenager. She smiles back so I guess she didn't pick up on the swears I was thinking in her direction. She opens the gate so I don't have to get off. I fall in behind Bailey and nudge NeeNee into trot. Now I know which is the inside rein, bend, and so on so I know which diagonal to rise on.

Elke is teaching someone else so Bailey and I have to stay out of the way. Still, at one point I see her watching me and when I cruise past on the correct diagonal, she says, "Looking goot, Lisa! Check your diagonal! A little squeeze on zuh outside rein unt ask for a bit more trot. See if you can keep her in zat frame."

Oh. Apparently I wasn't on the correct diagonal after all. But I don't dwell on it. Did she see my trot again? I think so! I have to admit NeeNee's head seems to be staying pretty steady, I don't think either of my reins is going loose-tight-loose-tight, and I'm practically giddy at the possibility I may know what *my trot* feels like! I should be able to get it again, sweaty feet in rubber boots notwithstanding.

Stormy Weather

AS IT TURNS OUT, THE next morning the skies are dark. By second period, it's pouring and the wind has picked up, lashing the rain against the classroom windows so hard it sometimes sounds like it could be hail.

I'm hardly able to concentrate on class, I'm so excited and nervous and giddy about Trent, but I realize I don't want to ride over to Elke's with a southeaster blowing. I'm considering doing it anyway, because once I'm there, I can ride in the indoor and get dried off before heading home again and if it means seeing Trent it would be worth it.

In the middle of fourth period, just before lunch, I get a text from Trent. *Call me when you can talk.* I'm studying it, trying to figure out if he wants to cancel, when I realize Mr. Zuck is standing right in front of me.

He asks, "I don't think you want me to take that away, do you?"

He doesn't look happy, but then, he never does. Who would, with a name like that? Imagine the jokes! But he's got a particularly cranky face right now so I don't think he's stewing about any of the variations of his name people use when he's out of hearing. He's either holding in a massive fart or he's annoyed at me. I'm pretty sure it's the latter, because he often leaves the lab on some pretext or other and I'm sure those absences are really just fart walks so he has no need to hold it in. One of the perks of being a teacher is that teachers can leave whenever they want. I quickly shove the phone back in my pocket and shake my head.

He goes across to the other aisle but turns to look at me again. He's going to ask me a question and I feel a little queasy because I suck at chemistry although it might not be bad if it wasn't for all the math, because I also suck at math. Thinking you suck at a subject is what Dad calls Having a Bad Attitude, and he's always going on about how Having a Bad Attitude is a Barrier to Learning. But then, he's an architect and he thinks math is fun, or what he calls Having a Positive Attitude. It's times like this I seriously wish I wasn't in the pre-matriculation program.

Fortunately, we're in chem lab so we don't have individual desks, and my lab partner, Maureen, is a Chemistry Ace. She actually works ahead of where we are in class, and she always does the extra marks questions on quizzes, she likes chemistry so much. She quietly pushes her notebook closer to me and you'd almost think it was an accident, her pen pointing to the answer like that. I'm able to read the answer, or at least enough of it that I don't seem to be a complete dud. I owe her some home-made cookies. Mom's, not mine. I suck at baking cookies too.

Mr. Zuck says, "Thank you, Maureen."

I feel my face turning red. When Mr. Zuck has gone on to his next question, strolling through the stations to see who's the least interested, intent on ruining someone else's morning, I whisper to Maureen, "Sorry."

She just shakes her head. I suppose it's a trial for her, having a lab partner like me. I like the experiments, though. I'm pretty good at adjusting the Bunsen burner, and I always say paradichlorobenzene instead of mothballs so I hope she's keeping that in mind. It's just a shame the topic of mothballs comes up so seldom now that everyone mostly wears synthetics because it's a very fun word to say and makes you look smart besides. I would point out that moth balls are now mostly naphthalene, which is also fun to say although it doesn't rise to the level of paradichlorobenzene.

Sometimes I think I should have been born German. They have lots of multi-syllabic words made by putting a bunch of other words together like *Bahnhofplatz* (train station place) *Parkplatz* (parking lot) and *Sitzplatz* (seat). I guess those are like the English words *dishwasher* and *fireplace*. If you don't know, *supercalifragilisticexpialidocious* is a made-up word so in my opinion it doesn't count even though you can find it in a dictionary, but we also have *antidisestablishmentarianism* which is a real thing and I doubt the Germans can beat that!

Anyway. The Warming Paradichlorobenzene Experiment was a couple of years ago and we're not doing it or any other experiment today, just getting ready for the one we're doing next, which doesn't sound very exciting. I'm pretty sure I already know everything I need to know about solubility. Dad would say thinking this way also falls into the category of Having a Bad Attitude.

The class finally comes to an end. As we're gathering up our books, Maureen says, "Was that your boyfriend who texted you?"

"No. Um, thanks for bailing me out."

She shrugs and says, "No problem. But you know, some teachers don't care much about phones but Mr. Zuck is *super* fussy about it."

"I know. But I don't think about it because no one ever texts me. Except Mom of course, and she only does it at lunch time." I know, it's pathetic admitting to someone you hardly know that you hardly know anyone. But Maureen seems to take it as a positive.

"Don't say it like it's a bad thing! Why does everyone spend so much time on their phones, anyway, instead of paying attention and actually *learning*?"

I study her face. She really means it. She needs to meet Jimmy!

"Hey," I say, "Do you go home for lunch? If not, would you like to have lunch with my friends and me? I mean, if you don't have other..."

"I'd like that," Maureen says so quickly she cuts me off. You'd think she's actually stoked about potentially becoming an Untouchable.

"Great! I'll save you a seat."

CALL ME LISA

MAUREEN FITS IN WELL and I'm glad I invited her. She isn't new at school, she doesn't haunt the halls always alone or anything like that, but she's sort of an outsider like me, only for different reasons. I'm not sure why I'm an outsider, maybe because I'm not like the popular girls who love shopping and being at the mall, which I can only stand so much of, even though I've mostly quit letting Mom buy my clothes. Maureen is pretty although she does wear quite a lot of eye shadow, and I thought, too much blush. (Turns out she has rosacea. Another reason not to make assumptions! But I'm getting ahead of my story.)

When I found out she was assigned to be my Chem Lab partner this year, I admit my first thought was, oh great, I'm saddled with a dummy, as if I'm ever going to burn up the track in chemistry. But I thought she must be dumb or possibly shallow just because of all that eye make-up and blush which turned out to not be blush. Probably the first week or maybe even the first day, I realized she's super smart and as you've already figured out, much better at chemistry than I am, better even that the smartest guy in our class which a lot of people would find astonishing. I think the only reason she isn't one of the populars is that she hasn't found any peers. It must be difficult to be brilliant and have to live your life surrounded by average people.

I'm very anxious to call Trent. I didn't want to call him before lunch because I wanted to make sure I was in the lunchroom when Maureen got there, and I don't want to call him with everyone hanging around and with all the noise, so now I'm in a hurry. I gulp down my all-time most favourite sandwich, tomatoes and spinach with Veganaise on sesame white even though you likely know it's a poor choice for an all-time, most favourite sandwich in one way: unless you eat it right after you make it, it's soggy. On the plus side, by lunch time al-though it is definitely soggy and can be messy, it does make for less chewing.

Anyway. The others take so long, gabbing and so on, I tell them I have to go, and leave before they're finished. Maureen and Jimmy get up when I do and walk out of the lunchroom with me, but when we're out the door, they peel off to go to his locker. He has some Grade Twelve chemistry practice tests he's willing to loan her. She must be giddy at the prospect. As I watch them walk away, I'm surprised to notice Jimmy is as tall as Maureen. Not that she's particularly tall, but last year she would have towered over him.

I go outside and walk a fair distance away from the smokers and vapers clustering under the canopy at the doorway in defiance of the signs, before calling Trent. Turns out he still wants to go to Elke's this afternoon but wonders if I'll ride over in such bad weather.

"You don't have to go, Trent," I tell him. "It's a lousy day to walk…"

"I know it's not that far but I could drive over."

"Oh, sure!" Why didn't I think of that? Duh!

"But you have to ride and it's a lousy day for that, too."

"They'll be riding in the indoor."

"Oh, they will? But you still have to ride over there. And I don't think it's a good idea."

"Umm, yeah." So. Looks like he's about to jam out.

"I just don't think it's safe, not in a storm like this. There's branches falling and stuff flying around everywhere." Well, he's right about that so as excuses go, it's a good one. But he doesn't want to jam out. He asks, "Do you ever go without your horse, just to watch or anything?"

"I, umm, yeah. No, not really."

"But could you? Wanna do that this afternoon, if it's still raining?"

"Oh, umm…" I'm wondering where this is going. Does he think I should walk over? Or drive maybe? That's probably it. He wouldn't know I haven't got my license yet. Most people my age do, after all. And Bailey rides, rain or shine, since she keeps her horse there. Aside from being a good excuse, it would be nice to watch her.

When I don't say anything for a moment, Trent suggests, "I could pick you up."

"Okay, then! That would be great!"

"Text me when you're ready to go."

"Okay."

"Talk to you later!" he says, and hangs up.

If I was Peony, I'd give a few Feel-Good Bucks. I actually have a Peony Feel-Good Buck imitation; it involves sort of arching my neck and emitting a little squeal as I prance, changing leads (now that I know what they are) at will. Full disclosure: I invented it when I was about ten, long before I had Peony, but I've mostly quit doing it. Still. If there ever was a time!

Today of course I restrain myself. I look like enough of an idiot as it is, standing three meters outside of the canopy getting soaking wet. I'm well aware of the guffaws from the smokers/vapers, which may be on account of an Untouchable too dumb to come in out of the rain, I don't know. I make eye contact with one of them briefly. He snorts and elbows the guy next to him so then that guy gawks at me too.

Who's the dummy here? They're standing under a glass canopy in the middle of a fierce rain and windstorm. The wind could whip around and rip the whole thing off although how that would kill any of them I don't know. If the gutter was blocked, there could be hundreds of liters of rainwater collecting in it and the weight could cause the whole thing to collapse on them. What if the glass broke into lethal shards? It would be a terrible disaster. Of course none of that happens, but it does make me feel superior knowing I'm smart enough not to stand under it.

I don't know why it takes mental pictures like that to make me feel superior to them anyway. They're idiots who laugh at farts after all. I lift my chin and sail right by.

Don't get me wrong, it's not that I don't think farts are funny. I can see how you might think that, after the Coop Incident and what I said about Mr. Zuck. Peony often farts when she's doing her Feel-Good Bucks as she goofs around in her paddock, and I think that's funny. It's only when someone yukky farts that I don't think it's funny. I guess not all the smokers are yukky. It's just Lisa Libra talking.

AS IT TURNS OUT, I don't go to Elke's or anywhere else with Trent. The storm is worse by dismissal time; heavy wind gusts knock down trees and powerlines. Luckily I don't miss the school bus and it makes it through the forested parts of the road without being detoured due to fallen trees, because just the five-minute walk from the bus stop to home and I am drenched. I'm barely in the door when somewhere near us something important gets knocked down and the power goes out.

A large branch in Trent's yard fell on his car. He wasn't in it at the time but until the branch is removed, no one is going in or out. I know this because he phoned instead of texting. He's in a dither. He says that he's done a lot of work on that car but it's old and not worth much, so he'll never get enough from the insurance company to replace what he had and they won't even consider repairing it because it would cost more than it's worth. Sad, right? He's hoping he can fix it himself, maybe he'll take it to the college and have the students work on it, or maybe he can get some help from the guy up the road who does frame off restorations. As soon as I have internet access, I'll find out what a frame off restoration is.

He says, "I can come over to your place on my dirt bike if you want. We could just hang out."

Hang out? It's going to be dark soon and if it's dangerous for me to be out in the storm, it's also dangerous for him.

"No, you're right, it's not safe. You go see about your car while there's still daylight. I'm going to feed my horse and then do some homework. Tomorrow is another day."

I played it cool, right? You know it's easier by phone than when you're face to face especially when there is a swoop of blonde-streaked hair and sparkling bright blue eyes involved. I'm hoping it makes up for me jabbering out that impulsive invitation yesterday.

"Tomorrow..." he says, just as my phone dies.

Tomorrow what? It sucks not being able to charge my phone and call him back to find out what he was going to tell me about tomorrow.

Anyway. Jemmy is engrossed in something on his tablet and has already helped himself to Cheetos to tide him over until Mom gets home. I make my all-time most favourite sandwich, peanut butter and dill pickle on multi-grain, get a glass of vanilla soy milk, and go upstairs with a couple of emergency candles. I get the candles set up on my desk ready to light when it gets dark enough I that need them and set to work on the Chemistry end-of-chapter quiz.

Well, I study it and I do make some headway but I get stuck on the second-last question. As usually happens whenever numbers and formulae are involved, it's like my brain has a Black Hole where they go to die.

The battery on my laptop is good for hours but cable is out, so no help from the internet. I give up and head downstairs. Jemmy is still on the couch in the family room.

"How're you doing?" I ask.

"Good." He doesn't look up.

"What're you doing?"

"Minecraft."

Okay, he's good for another hour at least, unless his tablet needs charging sooner.

One good thing about having a gas stove is that you can still cook when the power is off even though you have to light the burners manually. I can't text Mom to see if she wants me to start dinner. I think about waiting to see if she brings something home, like pizza maybe. The power can't be out all over town, after all. On the other hand, if she doesn't bring anything, it'll be kind of late to start cooking. I set about peeling potatoes which as you know can always be used another time should Mom bring a pizza. My Brownie Points must really be adding up.

She's back

UPDATE RE: ANGIE. SHE not only texts me back but comes over Sunday morning and sits on the tack trunk in the alleyway of the barn drinking her Serious Coffee Pumpkin Spice Latte while I get Peony tacked up. Normally she would have brought one for me even though they cost $3.99, that's how much she likes me, but I guess it slipped her mind today. I don't mention it.

Also normally, she would sit on the hay bales, but she doesn't today for two reasons: one, the tack trunk is closer to the crossties where I'm grooming Peony; and two, if she did, she'd likely end up with hay in her panties, her cut-off jeans are that cut off. I've had shavings in my jeans a couple of times due to misadventures I'd rather not describe, so I know how annoying that was and can only imagine how uncomfortable hay in your panties would be.

After a full ten minutes of Jarrett this and Jarrett that and Jarrett's friends are so cool and so on, finally she slows her torrent of words to take a sip of coffee. I think this may be a good time to update her on my progress with Peony, show-wise.

"Oh, you know," I start. But I left too big a space. I guess I shouldn't have put in a comma, because she continues as if I haven't spoken. This is something Jarrett always did. It looks like Angie has already spent enough time with him for at least one of his annoying habits to rub off.

"Jarrett's a *nice* guy, a *really nice* guy! He's *sweet* to me and everything, but sometimes..." Her thoughts seem to have been sucked out the door with her gaze.

I look out the doorway but can't figure out what drew her attention. I might try again to change the topic to Peony, but what's the point? She's not interested by the look of things. I prompt her with: "Sometimes what?"

"I dunno. It's just—well, I think he might have another girlfriend."

"Oh? Who?"

"I don't know."

"Maybe he's still dating Laurie Ann?"

"I don't think so."

"So what makes you think..."

"It's just, he's so up and down, you know, all attentive, and the next minute it's like I'm not even there. He keeps asking about you, his 'old friend', what you're doing, how are things on Saddle Ridge Way as if I'd know! And I don't like the way he looks at other girls. And there's been days, whole days, he hasn't even texted me or when he finally does, it's late. Once it was after I was asleep. When I asked him what he did that night, he blabbed something that really sounded like he was lying."

I take a stiff brush to the mud on Peony's fetlocks. She has quite a lot of hair there and of course it's white. In the old days I wouldn't have paid so much attention, but since I'm riding at Elke's, I want her to be as well-groomed as the horses that live there. It's no small task. Today it's welcome as it gives me time to ponder what Angie just said.

I have half a mind to ask her if she's ever seen the back of Jarrett's neck. I don't get her to read my stories anymore because she says they're Too Depressing and at times has mentioned she wonders what goes on in my head. You have to admit that story was not only Depressing but also Dark so it's definitely one she wouldn't like.

Because she hasn't read *Nikki and Jackson* she wouldn't understand the significance, would likely make some comment about I should know the difference between real life and my stories; my stories are just that: stories. Nobody lives in them and neither should I, and so on. If you're thinking she's said these things to me in the past, High Five to you. She's my best friend but sometimes she can be harsh. And she calls me judgmental! Besides, suggesting Jarrett is a snake would probably piss her off.

"He might be seeing someone else, I guess. You aren't like, exclusive, are you?" I ask instead.

"He hasn't asked me to go steady, but you know, it's just kind of expected, one girlfriend at a time."

"In what universe?" I brush the hair off my forehead with a hand, thinking I probably now have a smear of dirt there and will need to remember to wipe my face before I leave. I glance at Angie and see her down-turned mouth. I'm astonished. She thinks a few dates with Jarrett mean he's not going to date anyone else? And she expects him to account for his time when they're not together?

Now she's gushing on about Jarrett again, something about how silky the little patch of hair on his chest is, as if I need to hear about *that*. I tune her out and my thoughts wander. I've only ever had one real boyfriend. (Dwayne. If you're wondering, he had no hair on his chest, just silky smooth café-au-lait skin. But I digress.) I didn't expect him not to play the field, so called.

I try to summon how I would have felt if I thought Dwayne had another girlfriend. I like to think I'd just grit my teeth and try to out-do the competition somehow, maybe by being more fun or more interesting, or acting like I don't care. You know, I'd play it cool in hopes he'd end up choosing me. But then, Dwayne asked me to go steady almost as soon as we started dating. Of course, once he was a thousand kilometers away—well, we all know what happened after that.

Maybe Dwayne wanting to go steady so soon wasn't a good thing. Maybe we would still have a relationship, even long-distance, if we'd taken a little more time. You know, dated other people although that would be a challenge in my case, and worked into it gradually. More likely it was doomed from the start. Maybe being fickle is a natural condition of youth. I have to admit I'm not devastated by splitting with Dwayne but then I did have a couple of months to get used to the idea before it actually happened. Also, *Dylan*. Remember?

Angie doesn't answer the non-question about the universe. She looks so morose I decide against reminding her of their non-commitment status and just keep brushing, on the far side of Peony so I don't have to look at her. Or more to the point, so she can't see my face. I can't help it, I'm exasperated with her and I'm sure my expression shows it. Dad is fond of saying I'd never make a poker player.

"So anyway," she says loudly enough to make sure I can hear even with a horse between us, "you said you'd go to the skate bowl with me? How about this afternoon?"

"No, it's Sunday, remember? We have to go to the rescue."

"Well, I don't. I quit."

"You quit?"

"Yeah. It's dirty. And I have too much going on."

"You never minded the dirt before! And you're not going to go to the rescue even though you're not doing anything with Jarrett?" Am I trying to hurt her feelings? Maybe. But I think you'll agree she deserves it. I move around to the Angie side of Peony.

"I still might be, though. Doing something with Jarrett, I mean." If she's taken aback or even noticed my tone, she doesn't miss a beat. "He just hasn't asked me yet. I thought he might want to go and skate and maybe he thinks it's boring for me to sit there for such a long time. You know, like maybe it unconsciously makes him leave before he really wants to because I'm there." She gives me an intense look, easy when you have black eyes like hers, and nods as if that will make it so.

Oh sure, I think, nodding as if I agree, *maybe he's suddenly super considerate. Or maybe he's busy showing off for someone else.* But I say, "I, umm, can't go until later, because *I am* going to the rescue this afternoon. But I see why you can't. Jarrett might want to do something, and you need to keep your options open."

If she notices the sarcasm, she doesn't let on; she just nods and says, "Yeah. Later's okay."

"So I'll go with you. But right now, I need to hustle. I'm due at Elke's. Bailey's helping me. We're getting ready for the show."

"Okay, great! I'll come around seven? Or a little earlier? If he's not at the skate park, we might have to check out a couple other places."

"I don't want to be out late. School tomorrow, you know."

I'm a little hurt she hasn't picked up on my reminder about the show and disappointed she doesn't seem to feel guilty about quitting volunteering at the Mid-Island Horse and Donkey Rescue which if nothing else, means I need to find another way to get there. Jarrett must have some super power like Laurie Ann's Force Field Containment Spell. Maybe if you're a member of The Coven, you have that Super Power bestowed upon you! I'm beginning to see the attraction.

I push those thoughts away but can't stop the queasiness in my stomach. This could end up being a train wreck, depending on what Jarrett has going on. I hope he texts her and wants to do something with her, even though she'd be smart not to jump at a last minute invitation, in my opinion. I think she should tell him she's busy; she doesn't have to say busy with me and we wouldn't have to go to the skate bowl, so maybe he'd think she was seeing someone else, too, and it might smarten him up. If he is two-timing her, which I don't know, but if he is. But since I'm not a Jarrett fan and a novice in the boyfriend department besides, what I think doesn't count for much, and of course, she doesn't ask.

Then it occurs to me it could be Jarrett is only seeing Angie to make Laurie Anne jealous! For a second, I hope that's the case. And then I'm ashamed of myself for being such a small person. Also, if you have perceived the obvious flaw in my thinking which is that dating an Untouchable might be social suicide instead of making anyone jealous, High Five to you.

I don't know what's going through Angie's head but there's certainly no thought about playing hard to get. She looks happier than she has since she got here. She gets up off the tack trunk, tugs at the hem of her short shorts and says, "Great! I'll pick you up at six-thirty!" She drains her coffee, tosses her empty cup in the manure bucket by the crossties, turns and heads to her car in a big rush. Probably you have to get up to speed to break out of the Barn Time Warp Containment Field. Or it could be she got a little chill, sitting in the shade with all that bare skin. It is October, after all.

For a moment I watch her car cruise around the circular driveway and head for the road. I pull out my phone and text Alain to see if he can pick me up on his way to the Rescue. He responds a second later with a thumbs up emoji and 12:30. Thank you Alain. One problem solved.

Then my gaze falls on the cup in the manure tub. It's paper and will decompose in the manure pile, but I'll have to dig it out and take the plastic lid off. Angie has been here often enough to know where the recycling bin is.

First she presses me into service as her wing girl so she doesn't have to stalk Jarrett alone, and now this. Sometimes a girlfriend is as much trouble as a boyfriend.

Anyway. I finish tacking up, find a clean spot on the towel I use to clean mud off Peony's hooves and use it to wipe my face before putting my helmet on, then I take Peony to the fence I use since I don't have a mounting block, climb on and head for Elke's. I have to get my ride in and be back home in time for Alain to pick me up to go to the rescue.

BACK FROM THE RESCUE, I'm changing into clean jeans prepping for Skate Bowl Reconnaissance with Angie after dinner, when Dad calls. I ignore it. He leaves voicemail. I sink to my bed and listen to his message. He wants to take Jimmy and me for dinner tomorrow, which he reminds me is Monday. Like I'd forget. He wants me to let him know if that works for me.

I don't know how I feel about Dad. Mom hasn't said so, but I'm pretty sure their split is Dad's fault. You know, him being so distant which now seems like he was deliberately avoiding her. Avoiding all of us. I wonder if he had a secret life with a girlfriend and even maybe another family. I dread the thought of seeing him.

I go down to the kitchen. Mom and Jemmy are both there, engrossed in a discussion over whether Jemmy could eat Cheetos now and still have room for dinner. Mom says dinner will only be a few more minutes because the potatoes are almost done. Jemmy says he's so hungry he can't wait.

Mom is busy frying mushrooms to put alongside the potatoes and vegan breaded chicken cutlet. She looks up at me and says, "Good, you're here. Cut up some tomatoes and toss the salad, please." She pokes at the mushrooms with the pancake flipper. Everything's normal. Maybe seeing Dad won't be as traumatic as I'm imagining.

I come around to the counter where the lettuce and tomatoes await and set to work. After a moment, I casually say, "Dad wants to take Jemmy and me out for dinner tomorrow."

"Oh?" Mom says. "That's nice." She doesn't even look up.

Jemmy frowns, then brightens and says, "Could we go to Smitty's and sit by the aquarium?"

The last time we were at Smitty's, there was nothing vegan on the menu except for salad. I ordered a side of fries to go with it. It might have changed since then I suppose but call me selfish, I'd rather go where I know there's something I like.

"Maybe Milano's?" I suggest. "They don't have fish for you to watch but you could have pizza."

Jemmy thinks about it for a minute, then grins and says, "Okay!".

See? It's not really all that selfish of me, denying Jemmy the rapture of watching imprisoned koi swim listlessly back and forth, because he loves pizza.

"I'll tell him it's okay, then."

WE GET TO THE SKATE park just as Jarrett and his buds are leaving. Angie barely said a word to me all the way here and drove like a madwoman. She's pissed at me because she thinks I've made her late.

It was a long day, I'm tired, and I didn't want to come in the first place, so maybe I dawdled getting my purse, putting a little braid in my hair, I even washed my face and put on a Full Blast Make-up. I was hoping she might come to her senses. She didn't, it just annoyed her and she pointed out she's never seen me spend any time getting ready for anything before. She's right of course but all my piddling around only delayed the inevitable.

I don't have words to express how happy I am we got here alive, which is saying something since as you know, I have lots of words.

She has barely stopped the vehicle when she jumps out and runs to Jarrett. He picks up his skateboard and draws away from the other guys. I stay in the vehicle, watch her glom onto him like one of the bloodsuckers Jemmy often has on his legs when he comes back from the marsh, sickened at the sad spectacle and wishing I was anywhere else.

He gives her a quick hello kiss, then frowns as he looks my way. I shrink down in my seat but it's too late. He's seen me. He smiles and disentangles himself from Angie to give me a wave. It's a crying shame he's so good looking. Why couldn't he at least have giant ears or a big, hairy mole on his nose?

He starts toward me but Angie grabs his arm and turns him to face her. He pulls his arm out of her grasp and scratches the back of his neck as they have a discussion. I imagine the new scales erupting there are probably itchy. Then Angie comes back to the vehicle, gets in, and starts the engine.

"What's up?" I ask.

"Jarrett's going to come and pick me up at my place. We're all going over to Gavin's to play video games." She doesn't look at me and it's clear she's still mad, which is totally unfair. She should be pleased because now she'll get her wish: Jarrett, tonight.

A few months ago, playing video games was something she slammed a guy she was dating for, and now she's all in a dither to get on with it? But she's right, I don't want to go, and I'm surprised her super strict parents are okay with it. I ask, "It's kind of late. Do your folks let you go out on school nights now?"

"I'm *eighteen!*" she snaps, as if somehow being eighteen explains it. The tires spray gravel as we leave the parking lot in a plume of dust. This can easily happen because the entrance area is quite steep. It's too bad the City used up the entire skate bowl budget before paving the parking area. But if it was paved, I suppose the skaters would be all over it and then no one would be able to park there. I wonder about the steep access to the street...maybe if it was paved and a skateboarder came zooming up full speed and in the middle of a Casper Disaster or Coconut Wheelie, goes too far out into the road where a truck...

"Don't worry," she says, breaking into my reverie, "I knew you wouldn't want to go, so I'm dropping you off at your place first. So you put on make-up for nothing." She says this in a snarky tone and gives me a sideways look. It's her way of saying she knows I was procrastinating. It's just as well she interrupted my thoughts because I have no idea whether either of those skateboarding tricks I mentioned would actually work on the incline to the road. They are just two tricks I've heard the boys talk about that I like the sound of.

I'm relieved for two reasons: one, I don't have to go to Gavin's; and two, she didn't abandon me at the skate park. Just everywhere else.

Something Special

SHE TAPS HER FOOT. Clicks her tongue. Leaps to her feet and strides from the bench to the edge of the tennis court and back, then delivers a half-hearted blow to her sport bag with the racquet. It's getting dark and the court lights are coming on. Pam is late again and soon their court time will be up. Some guy must have come along. Doesn't even have to be a special guy. To Pam, any guy is something special.

Pam wasn't home from work when they needed to leave to be at the park for their court time, so Hillary left without her. If Incredible Edibles is busy, Pam can't always leave right at the end of her shift so she occasionally takes her tennis things with her. That way she can change at work and come straight to the park. Hillary didn't see her leave and doesn't know if she took her duffle bag this morning, so that could be it. But Pam usually sends a text.

For the tenth time, Hillary checks her phone for messages. Still nothing. She rams her racquet into its press, snaps it tight, picks her bag up off the bench and walks along the chain link fence to the gate.

"I guess my friend isn't going to make it," she says to the couple waiting for the court, "you can have the rest of my time." They thank her and hold the gate until she's through.

As she walks toward the parking lot, calls from a group of guys playing soccer on the nearby pitch attract her attention. The ball, kicked wildly out of play, bounces through the stand of native firs and rolls toward her. She stops it with a foot.

One of the soccer players breaks away from the group and trots toward her. She kicks the ball to him.

He stops it and calls out, "Thanks!" Then he smiles, takes the hem of his T-shirt and pulls it up to wipe sweat from his brow. She is treated to a view of his six pack. Maybe that was the idea.

"You're welcome," she responds, then turns away.

"Hey!" he calls.

She turns around. Instead of rejoining his friends, the guy has moved closer.

"Hey," he says again, juggling the ball on his toe, "we're a couple of players short. Wanna kick the ball around for a while?"

"Um, no. Thanks, though."

"No?" He turns and drop kicks the ball to his friends on the pitch, then turns back to her. "You're right, it's not a game so it doesn't matter how many guys we have. I was just...Well, my name's Eric. Your boyfriend stand you up?"

"No."

"So you came here just to bash the ball against the backboard for half an hour?"

He's cute. His eyes have a twinkle. She feels a tug of interest, then reminds herself this park is near where all those girls have disappeared and Ted Bundy was good-looking with an engaging smile, too. She thinks, *I should walk away*. Instead, she musters a polite smile and says, "Not my boyfriend. Just a friend."

"Some friend," he says. "I like tennis. More than soccer, actually. It's just that none of my friends play. Wish I brought my racquet, I'd've joined you."

"Sure," Hillary says; she shrugs, then turns and walks away.

"Hey!" he calls after her, "I'll come again tomorrow, same time! I'll bring my racquet!"

Without turning, she waves back over her shoulder.

"SO, PAM, WHAT HAPPENED to you last night?" Hillary asks. She fills two mugs with coffee and puts them on the table next to the Cinnaswirl. "You know I was waiting for you! I hung around the tennis court looking like an idiot for half an hour and I must've texted you ten times. Couldn't you have let me know you weren't going to show up?"

"Sorry, Hill," Pam says. She dumps Cinnaswirl into her coffee and sticks her nose in the mug, drawing in cinnamon coffee smells before slurping noisily. "Mmmm. Needed this."

"Well?"

"Greg Lindeman, remember him? He's so cute! He saw me at the bus stop and picked me up. Invited me to a party. We just went straight there."

"Good effin' god, Pam!"

"I know! I wasn't exactly dressed for it. I wanted to go home and change but Greg said the cashier-girl look was kind of a turn on."

"That's not what I meant!" Hillary blows out a breath and shakes her head. She feels rage surge through her. She rises from her chair so quickly it slides back on the linoleum and nearly tips.

Pam looks up from her coffee. "You're mad," she observes.

"Yeah, I'm mad! Don't you think you'd be mad if I did that to you? You couldn't even send me a text, FFS?"

Pam presses her lips together and juts out her chin. Hillary has seen that look on her roommate's face often enough to know there's no point talking to her. She picks up her mug but instead of sitting down again, goes to the counter and leans back against it, frowning angrily at Pam. Pam doesn't notice because she doesn't look up. They drink their coffee in stony silence.

Then Pam gets unsteadily to her feet and says, "Jeez, I think I'm still drunk. I'm going back to bed." She takes the few steps toward the hall, then turns back and says, "Greg said he might be at the Laughing Oyster tonight. I need you to come with me."

"Why?"

"I can't go alone! What if he's not there yet? I'll look..."

"Well, I don't want to go," Hillary cuts her off. "I can't afford it, for one thing. Besides, guys you meet at the bar are guys who drink, and half of them are married to boot. There has to be a better way."

"Like what? Friday nights at the park playing tennis with me? Besides, what's wrong with guys who drink? A person can like drinking without being an alcoholic or anything. You had a good time last time we went."

"Sure. Until that guy paid your bar tab and you left me there."

"Your own fault, Hill. His friend would've been happy to pay your tab."

"I didn't like the cost."

"Tick tock tick tock. You know what that is? It's the sound of your biological clock ticking. Looks don't last forever. Not even yours."

"At least I like what I see in the mirror."

Pam's eyes narrow and her nostrils flare as she draws a deep breath and straightens her shoulders. "You know what? You think you're something special? You just keep on thinking that and before you know it what you see in the mirror will be an ugly old bag." She turns and disappears down the hall. Her bedroom door slams.

When she replays the conversation in her mind Hillary feels a twinge of remorse. Maybe she owes Pam an apology. When Pam wakes up, maybe she'll tell her she's changed her mind and will go to the pub with her tonight.

She pours a fresh cup of coffee, tops it up with Cinnaswirl, and takes it into the living room. There's a pond of sunlight on the armchair next to the window, and she sinks into it. Bright specks of dust float out of the sunbeam, then disappear.

As the sun warms her, she lets her mind play back over her conversation with that guy at the park yesterday. Eric, he said his name was. He *was* cute. If she went back to the park later today, would he really be there with his racquet?

These are her choices: go to the pub with Pam, or go to the park and see if Eric is there. *If I'm having this much trouble deciding, I must not like either option*, she thinks. *I'll just stay home. There are worse things than being alone.*

But sometimes, on a Saturday night, it doesn't feel like it.

WHAT DOES HILLARY DO? Does she go to the pub? Meet some great guy? Or does she go to the park and hook up with Eric? Does he turn out to be a total jerk? Or maybe he's great?

It's up to you. Write an ending you're happy with, because that's all I have. If I knew where it went from there, I would have written a better ending myself.

Have you guessed who Hillary and Pam are? If so, High Five to you.

Frosty

HAVE YOU FORGOTTEN about Trent? It's been a while since I mentioned him, and maybe you're thinking I sent him on his exploration voyage. You can forget about that! Even though I think he's with Nicole and I explained all the reasons he wouldn't trade her for me, he is still in the Potential Boyfriend Pool. Or more accurately, the Potential Boyfriend Slightly Damp Pothole.

He has texted me twice since I saw him with Nicole on Saturday. Just 'Hi' and a Happy Face Emoji, to which I naturally responded in kind. Now it's Monday after school, I'm on the way to Elke's, and he's waiting for me on the road in front of his place.

As I ride up, I see him smiling and get a warm feeling all over. He's not in his lumpy clothes, just jeans that are snug enough there's no danger he might accidentally moon someone if he has to tie his shoe, and a short-sleeved T-shirt with Monty's Motorcycles logo emblazoned across it. A beam of autumn sunlight breaks through the clouds and makes his hair glow like he's wearing a halo. You'd feel warm all over if he smiled at you, too.

"Hi, Lisa!" he calls out. He runs a hand through his forelock to sweep it away from his face.

"Hi!" That came out nice and friendly-sounding and without squeaking. So far so good.

He comes to walk beside us. "Such a beautiful horse," he says. "Suits you."

"Oh, umm, thanks." Was that a compliment? To me? Now I'm frazzled. I decide to push it out of my mind. I don't want to say something stupid, like telling him he's beautiful too, so I have to be careful because as you know sometimes things come out of my mouth unexpectedly.

"Okay if I go with you today?"

Okay? More than okay! I say, "Sure, I guess." As surprised as I am at this positive turn of events, I think I'm playing it pretty cool.

As we pass his driveway, I look toward the house and see his car in front of the garage. "Oh, there's your car. I thought it was totaled."

"Yeah, it is. Cost to fix it is more than it's worth, so they call it a *constructive* total loss. The tree hit the driver's side. It's dented and the roof's out of kilter, tough to open the driver's door, but luckily it's still driveable. Just needs some body work. I'm thinking of taking it to the body shop at the college."

"Oh." He wasn't lying about his car being wrecked after all, so no deception there. If you think I feel a rush of relief, High Five to you! There's still the question of Nicole, of course.

"Anyway," he continues, "I can work on it. It's not all bad. The cash payout from insurance'll be enough to cover anything I have to buy." He strides along beside us, giving me ample opportunity to see the top of his head (thick hair with no evidence of nits or even dandruff) and the back of his neck (no scales).

"How was your week-end?" I ask. "I mean, your events and so on."

"Not bad on Saturday. The track was muddy so no one was going to break any records. I was middle of the pack, tenth in my group."

"That doesn't sound bad. How many in your group?"

"Um, thirty-seven."

"Top ten isn't middle of the pack, then, Trent! It's great!"

"Yeah, not bad I guess."

I notice the back of his scale-less neck is turning pink. My god, he's downplaying how well he did, and he's blushing! I think I'm in love.

"Yeah, well. Anyway, on Sunday, I made friends with the mud."

"Umm, you made friends with the mud? What do you mean?"

"It means the mud and I got real close. The nice thing about mud is that it's softer than dirt."

"Oh, you crashed?"

"Yeah."

"You okay?"

"My shoulder's a little sore today, that's all. Shoulda heard my buddies laughing, once they found out I wasn't hurt. I had liquid mud dripping off me. I guess it was pretty funny. And when I got home, I found mud in places you'd never expect. But the worst thing is that besides having my car to fix, now I've got work to do on my bike, too."

"Oh. That's too bad."

He shrugs and looks up at me with a smile. I notice he has an eye tooth slightly out of alignment. It doesn't detract from his smile, though, not even a little bit. "Between classes and my job, I don't have a lot of time. It'll be the old quad for me for a while I guess. What about your show, the show you said you're getting ready for?"

"I'm working on my tests. I'm doing Training Level Tests One and Two, which won't mean anything to you. My friend Bailey is going to help me with them and we'll run through parts this afternoon so if you can stand to stay that long, you can find out for yourself if dressage is as boring as watching paint dry."

"Great! So the show—it's Saturday?"

"Yes."

"Where and when?"

"It's Saturday at Beban Park. Free to attend!" I chuckle to cover up how dumb that comment was. As if he'd want to go and watch! I rush on: "I haven't got my ride times yet. They'll let me know in a day or two. We'll be taking the horses over first thing in the morning because we have stalls for them there and we'll take hay for them and some kibble for their lunch and we'll stay most of the day." OMG Lisa, you're running off at the mouth like a complete idiot! Put in a Full Stop or at least a Comma somewhere!

I concentrate on keeping my mouth shut and we walk quietly for a few moments, the only sounds the rhythmic kaplop kaplop of Peony's feet when she wanders up onto the pavement, and one lengthy but quiet fart (Peony's, not Trent's). Finally, I think to ask him about school.

"Umm, you mention a job. And classes. I haven't seen you at school."

"I'm up at VIU."

"Ohhh! What are you taking?"

"Everything!" He barks out a laugh. "Everything and nothing. I guess I'll get a B.A. I have no idea why I'm even there, I don't have a clue what I want to do. My Dad's a doctor so of course he thinks I should be working on a B.Sc. but I'm really not into it. I like mechanics, mechanical things, more than people."

"Maybe you'll figure something out before you graduate. But you could take some of the, um, engine courses too."

"We'll see, I guess. Dad's really not what you'd call enthralled with the idea, though. He thinks engine grease and moving parts should never be near a doctor's hands."

"What does your mom think?"

"She's on my side, mostly just to take a position in opposition to Dad's. That's what Dad thinks, anyway." He kicks a pebble off the pavement. "She lives in Ontario."

"Oh."

"She's originally from there, went back after they split. She's really into politics. Now she's married to the MP from Etobicoke."

"You didn't go with her?"

"They left the decision up to me. I think Mom was pretty relieved when I decided to stay with Dad. So here I am! We used to live in Sayward. Dad had a chance to get into a practice in Nanaimo so we moved here when I finished grade twelve. Works out, because we're close to VIU."

"So you haven't been in Nanaimo very long. Sounds like you've made friends already and you've even got a job."

"Yeah, I work at Buy Low Foods, part time of course. So there's a couple people there I guess are friends, not that we hang out really. There's a couple from dirt biking and a couple from class. Hey, you know the girl that lives across the street from us, Nicole?"

Grrr! Here it comes, I think. "Yeah, um, I've known her since we were in grade eight."

"She came over and introduced herself as soon as we got here. Even before we had time to unpack."

"She's very friendly." That's all I can think of to say. I'm quiet for three or four of Peony's steps, then I add, "She's very pretty, too."

"Yeah."

My shoulders slump. Did I think he would say she's not?

"She used to have a horse," I continue, "but I guess she outgrew horses, you know, the horse craziness."

"I wouldn't call it craziness, just an interest," he says, but doesn't elaborate further. After an uncomfortable lapse in the conversation during which I'm wracking my brain trying to think of something to ask him about himself or to tell him about myself that would make me seem interesting, he asks, "How about you?"

"Well, I still have the *interest*, as you can see," I say, and pat Peony's withers. Then I jabber on, spewing all there is to know about Lisa Rogney, probably more than anyone would ever want to know. Fortunately I manage to hobble my lip before I tell him my favourite colour is puce (it's not! It's sort of the colour of puke when your mother gave you Pepto Bismol to settle your stomach but it didn't work. Appropriate? Puce/Puke? I just like saying the word even though it's only one syllable). I have the remarkable restraint to stop short of telling him I wear size eleven shoes and a thirty-two A bra. Still, before I know it, I'm telling him about my parents splitting up.

"I'm really sorry, Lisa. It's tough." He reaches out and gives my thigh a little pat. "It's awful at first, but it gets better."

(Is patting my thigh a little too familiar? Keep in mind it's all he could reach, other than my rubber boot.)

"Thank you." My voice is barely more than a whisper. I'm ambushed by unexpected sadness. I blink furiously to keep back the tears and look off across the ditch to where a little red-breasted bird is hopping along in the fallen leaves under the bushes, foraging. *Spotted Towhee*, I think. Thanks, Jemmy.

When we get to the outdoor ring at Elke's a few minutes later, he opens the gate and I ride through. Bailey is just coming out of the barn, Dressage Canada Omnibus in hand. She crosses the paved area and comes to the gate, so Trent holds it open for her, too.

"Hi Bailey! This is Trent."

They say their how-do-you-do words and some kind of small talk ensues as I point Peony down the rail, pick up trot since we've done plenty of walk warm-up just getting here, and go all around the ring, making a few circles and walk-trot-walk-trot transitions here and there. When I'm back at the gate, Bailey gives Trent a smile and tells him he's welcome to come inside and sit on the mounting block to watch if he wants to. He's unaware of the honor just bestowed upon him and elects to stay outside the fence.

There are a couple of other riders in the near end of the ring, so Bailey suggests we go to the far end, and Bailey heads that way.

"Let me check your girth," she says when we get there. She sticks the omnibus in her armpit to free her hands and fuss unnecessarily with the buckles on the girth, and asks in a hushed voice, "Where did you find the *hunk*?"

"He's my neighbour."

"Why wasn't he at your party?"

"Well, I only met him a few days ago."

"And already he's come to watch you ride."

"Yeah, that's nice, right?"

"Right. Very nice. But don't expect it to last. Boyfriends all do that at the beginning."

"He's not my boyfriend!" This comes out in a sort of quiet hiss. Not that I'm mad. Just embarrassed.

"Oh no?" Bailey looks up at me with a teasing twinkle in her eye. "Not yet, you mean. Judging by how he was looking at you, I'd say he'd like to change that!"

I feel heat rising up my face and for once I'm speechless, maybe because it's difficult to speak when your lips are stretched into such a cartoonishly-huge smile. I hope she's right. I hope she's seeing something I don't. And then I remember Nicole. I'm about to tell her how I've seen her with him a few times, when Bailey says, "Anyway, let's get to work. I'm meeting Coop at five so I don't have a lot of time. What would you say is your biggest concern with your tests?"

I pull my mind off of what she said about Trent with difficulty, think about her question for a second, and say, "Probably the free walk. Every time I try to get her to put some energy into it, she jogs. Also when I pick up the reins again, she thinks it means trot."

"Okay. I think the free walk comes after the medium walk." She studies the omnibus and says, "How about this? Start with the fourth movement. Do your twenty meter canter circle at B, get your working trot just before you get back to B, and medium walk at C. Then around the corner to H in a nice marching medium walk, and across the diagonal."

Bailey walks along beside and coaches me through the letting out and picking up of the reins. "Remember, you're going away from the judge. You should have your reins up nicely so you're ready for your medium walk again at F because you need to prepare so you can get your up transition to trot at A, and you don't want to be fussing with the reins where she can see you. And from now on, don't start into trot as soon as you pick up the reins. *Always always always* walk a few strides on the bit first, even if you're out on the trail, because otherwise you're teaching her that picking up the reins means trot."

I agree to do as she says, and then we run through the movement a few times, try some transitions to left lead canter, and before I know it, she's saying it's been nearly an hour and she has to go. I'm ready to quit for the day, too, so I follow her out the gate. I look around but I don't see Trent. I wonder when he left. I guess Coop is right, watching is boring.

I ride out onto the tarmac and spot Trent in the alleyway of the barn, chatting with Elke. He looks up, smiles, and says something that leaves Elke smiling after him as he comes toward me.

"Ready to go?" he asks. I say I am, and we start back home.

"Sorry I didn't see the end of your ride. I really wanted to take a look at the horses in the barn. Man, are they something! Such beautiful animals! I don't think there's any as big as Peony, though."

"Elke's horses are as big, but they're in her own barn."

"She seems very nice. Good looking, too. Is she married?"

"Yeah."

"Too bad. I think my Dad would like her."

I'll admit it, my first thought was that Trent might be interested in her, you know, the Mystique of The Experienced Older Woman, because as I mentioned, she is very beautiful. Sometimes runaway thoughts are a curse.

I'm struggling for something to say when he comes out with, "Hey, you like Frosties? I love them. Might even be addicted. They're on for ninety-nine cents. Wanna go get one?"

"I've never had a Frosty."

"No time like the present."

"Sure!"

"Okay! I'll get my car and come to your place." He trots off ahead.

It's a date? It's a date! I might swoon if I wasn't worried about falling off. It's a long way down. So instead I pick up the reins and remember to walk a few strides before I nudge Peony into a trot.

I get to the barn and put Peony away in record time. I really want to change into something less horsey and sweaty before Trent shows up, so I don't have time to waste. I'm just closing the tack room door when I hear a car drive into the yard. Maybe he'll understand if I ask him to wait a few minutes.

I hurry out of the barn and stop in my tracks. The car I heard isn't Trent's or at least it isn't only Trent's. His car is here, just behind Dad's. They're both getting out of their cars.

As I walk toward them, they shake hands. When I reach them, Dad is telling Trent about his in-line six cylinder transversely mounted engine. Trent asks to see it.

Dad turns to me and says, "Hi, Lisa! You ready to go?"

"N...n...no. I just got back from Elke's. I need to change."

"Okay, take your time. See if Jemmy's ready, okay?"

I nod, so he goes around to the driver's side to lean in and unlatch the hood.

Are you thinking he should have given me a hug, since I haven't seen him since he left? I'm not surprised. He's not a huggy kind of guy.

"I'm sorry, Trent," I say. "I completely forgot Dad was taking us to dinner tonight."

"It's okay, Lisa, it's all good. We can get that Frosty anytime." He gives my arm a rub, then busies himself lifting the hood.

I stand for a moment, obviously dismissed, so I head for the house to change.

Dad and Trent are half bent over the fender of the car, discussing the finer points of the marvelous in-line, six cylinder, transversely-mounted engine when I come back out. I know I didn't take that long to change, no makeup or little hair braid, maybe five minutes? But even so, they're still drooling over the engine, for Pete's sake? I don't think I'll ever understand how anyone can look at an engine that long, in-line what's it or not. They barely notice me.

Mom made Jemmy wash up, but now he comes flying out the back door and rams Dad from behind. He turns and pulls his son into his arms. Jemmy, the kid who doesn't want to be hugged, is hugging the dad who isn't huggy, tight. I watch for a second, then take a deep breath and turn away.

I must be a terrible daughter to forget my date with my Dad but all I'm thinking is that missing out on my first Frosty and I don't even get a hug.

IF YOU'RE THINKING our dinner might be kind of awkward, High Five to you! I guess that's normal. This is all new to us and will take some getting used to.

"Don't worry, guys," Dad says as we wait for our food, "we'll see a lot of each other. I'm living in Hawthorne Heights, so it's not that far away. We've got three bedrooms, so you'll each have your own bed when you come for an overnight."

We've got three bedrooms? There's a *we*?

Jemmy doesn't notice the *we* and asks, "You said there's a marsh?"

"Yeah! It's close to one, anyway. Buttertubs. I think you went there on a school field trip"

"Oh yeah! Cool!" Jemmy squirms and I have a fleeting concern it might be because of something he has in his pocket. "I can go all the time, then!"

"I don't want you to go there alone, though, at least until you're older."

"Awww!"

"Really. It might not be safe."

"How come?"

"Well, you never know what could happen. It's deeper than our marsh. What if you fell in?"

"Oh. I can swim, you know."

"I know. But I'd feel better if someone went with you. Lisa could go with you. Or my friend and I will."

Friend? I don't know what he reads in my face, but he studies me for a heartbeat, then says, "My friend lives in the condo, too."

"Oh," Jemmy pipes up, "like you're having a sleepover, but all the time!"

"That's right, Jemmy." He smiles, but now he's avoiding eye contact with me.

It's another of those times it would be nice to be ten, huggable and innocent, again.

Sehr Goot

ELKE IS IN THE MIDDLE of the ring. Yes, it's an unscheduled lesson. I signed up for an extra one to prepare for the show. My saddle fund is depleted after that trip to the tack shop I mentioned, so fifty bucks won't make a big difference.

I'm concentrating on riding a perfect twenty-meter circle around her. It's more difficult than you might imagine, especially when it's trot for a quarter of the circle, walk for a quarter circle, trot for a quarter circle, and so on. Then we switch it up to walk five steps, trot for a quarter circle. Then three walk steps, trot for a quarter circle.

"Zere are no corners on a circle, Lisa," Elke says. "Don't pull her around wiss your inside rein. Bend her around your inside leg unt use zuh outside rein against her... Not like zat! On her wizzers. Hands down! Don't push down on zuh reins. No piano hands! Sumbs on top. Don't let her outside shoulder bulge out like zat! Half halt zuh outside rein unt moof your inside leg back a little on zis rein to stop her haunches from falling in. More inside leg! Push her out wiss your inside leg unt catch her on your outside rein. Half halt! Don't let her run! Inside leg to outside rein alvace. Don't stay on zuh rail, just touch zuh track at B und E, no riding along zuh rail! Zat's not a circle if it has flat spots." And so on. Honestly, sometimes I can't listen fast enough.

Elke decides I need help knowing how big a twenty-meter circle is, so she goes to the pylons stacked next to the mounting block and brings four of them to put out around the circle. There's only about a meter between the pylons and the fence at B and E. If you're wondering where the Gremlin Bush is, High Five to you! It's right on the other side of the fence at B and if I ride outside of the pylon we will obviously be within gremlin striking distance. But this is no time to pretend I don't know what Elke is telling me to do. Thankfully the Gremlin is not in residence today, or at least NeeNee doesn't think so.

"Okay now, keep outside uff zuh pylons. Don't let her slam on zuh brakes ven you vaunt zuh vok transition. *Forward* to vok! Keep! Both! Legs! On!"

I should point out I do have both legs on, just not as strongly as is needed I guess. I don't want you to blame Peony, even though she is good at ignoring me when I ask for trot so it's a challenge to get just the three walk steps Elke wants. You have to keep in mind Peony is just learning this stuff too.

Elke watches as we make a couple of circles on the outside of the pylons. "Goot! Now make zuh circle inside zuh pylons by pushing her in wiss your outside leg. Gradually, not just of a sudden! Take a quarter uff zuh circle to do it. Goot! Now push her back out. Keep your legs on! Outside shoulder back! Drop your weight into your heels. Legs on!"

It goes without saying all this stuff is spread out and not just jabbered in a non-stop list like I'm telling it, and there's a whole bunch more she's saying in between. It's exhausting, for Elke too I imagine. Her voice would be shot by the end of the day if she had to yell all this but she has a little microphone and I have a little earpiece so she doesn't have to talk very loud because it's right in my ear. Nice for Elke but it does mean I can't pretend I can't hear her even at the far end of the ring.

I suppose she doesn't have to keep nattering away at me, but then, what would be the point of having a lesson, right? The way I figure it, if she didn't have all these corrections to keep firing at me, I wouldn't be getting my fifty bucks worth. I'm looking forward to the day there aren't quite so many, just the same.

"Okay now, ziss time ven you ask for zuh transition, push her back to zuh outside unt ven you feel a good moment unt she's nice unt round on zuh outside rein, instead of asking for vok, a little half halt unt slip zuh canter aid on."

I do it. Peony picks up left lead canter like a charm.

"Goot!" Elke calls out. "Stay on zuh circle! Outside shoulder back! Let her canter! Ven you are back at B, ask for trot. Goot! Now slip zuh canter aid on again! Goot! Another circle now! Now trot!"

We keep on with these trot-canter-trot-canter transitions for another few times around the pylons, then Elke says, "Sehr goot! Vok unt let her haff a long rein. Ve take a break unt zen same sing on zuh uzzer rein."

I thought I was pretty fit what with all the stepping I do, but I'm breathing hard and sweating nearly as much as Peony. We both welcome the break. Don't ever let anyone tell you the horse does all the work!

Elke watches for a moment, takes a phone call, then comes back and says, "So, Lisa, if you can remember vut ve doing for zuh canter circles on your test, you'll do fine! You haff between K unt A to pick up left lead canter. Use zuh corner to get her bent around your inside leg nicely unt just like you did here, quietly slip zuh aid on. No big deal. Don't get busy doing funny sings wiss your hands! No drama."

"What if I get the wrong lead? Do I just leave it..."

"Ach, no! Not only zuh judge but everyone vatching vill notice. You don't vont zem to sink you don't know vot lead you're on! Much better to fix it. If you get zuh wrong lead, trot unt try again. If you make a mistake, any mistake, anywhere in zuh test, you *must* put it out of your mind! It's only vun movement. Don't let it spoil zuh rest of your test!"

"I'll try," I agree.

"Don't vurry. I'll be zere unt I'll help you varm up."

"You will?" I ask, surprised she would want anyone to know someone as inept as I am is her student.

"But of course!" she says. "Now, ven you're ready, back on zuh circle, same sing on zuh right rein. Unt zen ve will run through zuh entire test."

So that's what we did.

I have to mention something Elke said at the end of my lesson: "You vill do fine! Peony iss a nice mover unt you ride her vell unt she's a sehr goot fit for you. You haff a sehr goot rider's body, a nice long leg, goot for dressage."

First of all, I'd like to point out both my legs are long, but this is the first time in my life I've thought they were good for anything besides making it hard to buy jeans. I know I'm bragging, and bragging is not a nice quality in a person, but my legs are not ridiculous, but good? Who knew! If I had doubts about being a dressage rider, they just evaporated.

I SHOULD MENTION HERE that I'm not trying to make fun of Elke's accent or the fact she frequently mixes in German words. I'm not. In fact I think it's charming, and it suits her. I'm just writing it the way she says it because I think it will help to set the stage for you, and also, so you can see why sometimes I legitimately might not understand what she's telling me to do.

I'VE SPENT TOO LONG in the library so I miss the bus. I call Mom to see if she can pick me up. She says she's taking Jemmy to karate and I can go over and meet her at the dojo if I want a ride. I decline and set off on foot.

It hotter than usual for October, but there are two good things to keep in mind: one, the shady stretch through the forest is cool and welcome; and two: I bet I get even more than ten thousand steps each way.

As I approach the highway crossing I see the red car with the spoiler waiting for the light. There's a passenger. She turns her face my way and for a moment our eyes meet. Her face twists in an expression of triumph and before the light changes and the traffic moves off she flips me the bird and sticks her tongue out at me.

I know it shouldn't bother me. One little outing over to Elke's and an invitation to go for a Frosty is really no reason to think Trent is interested *interested* in me, no matter what Bailey says. I already explained why no guy would prefer me over Nicole. So why do I have this little stomach squeeze right now?

There is one thing that's sort of a bright spot or if you prefer, something to feel superior about: Nicole must have told me a hundred times sticking my tongue out was childish, and now she sticks hers out? When I next see her I'll mention it, in a clever way like: "I'm worried about those spots on your tongue" or something like that. Of course I couldn't see any spots from that distance, but you know, just a follow-up to Angie's famous put-down from last spring.

Thinking about Angie makes me realize how much I miss her. I decide to text her, whether or not she ever texts back. Maybe I'll suggest I wouldn't mind going with her if she's meeting Jarrett somewhere, even if it's at the skate bowl. Yes, I'm willing to do that, just to be with Angie.

Another thing I think about is whether I can speak in a believable German accent. I've heard enough of how Elke speaks to think I can emulate it. I have the path to myself, so I give it a try. I sink it verks out sehr goot. So goot that when an Intense Jogger Mother pushing a stroller with two babies in it comes my way, I say: "Gooten abend! Schmects goot!"

She smiles and acknowledges my greeting with a lift of her chin so she doesn't have to quit jogging even though you'd think she'd welcome the excuse for a break, sweating and huffing and puffing as she is.

When I think about it later, I realize I may have said "good evening" in the middle of the afternoon, and then told her she tastes good. Or maybe smells good? Or possibly it means let's eat. Perhaps I should stick with German-accented English.

JIMMY SPENDS A LOT of time at our place. You know he likes Jemmy, but he also hangs with Mom when she's baking cookies or just drinking (coffee or wine, depending on the time of day). When Dad was still here, he spent time polishing things with him. I think the whole family idea is attractive to him. When I remember where he came from, it makes sense.

I haven't given much thought to how he feels about Mom and Dad breaking up. Why would I? But when I hoof it up the driveway and see his bike leaning against the garage wall, I realize he's affected by it too. His father has been in jail since he was a little kid, and he spent more time with my Dad than any of the rest of us did. He might miss him more than I do.

He's waiting at the table on the patio with a text book open in front of him. Mom and Jemmy aren't home from karate yet and obviously I'm late getting home from school, so Jimmy can't get in the house. I think it's time we gave Jimmy the code for the lock. I make a mental note to mention it to Mom.

"Hey," I say, "sorry I'm late. Been waiting long?"

"Not long. Maybe ten minutes."

"You know this is Jemmy's karate day."

"I know, but I thought your dad was taking him."

"Mom thought so too until he texted with some excuse this morning."

"Hmmm. Jemmy will be disappointed." He shakes his head slowly before continuing, "Well anyway, when they get home, we're going down to the marsh. Dunno if we'll find frogs at this time of year, but just going there..." he shrugs as his words trail off.

"You're a sehr goot *Freund*."

He looks perplexed for a second, then says, "*Danke*, so are you."

"I think I would be a *Freundin*."

"I think you're right," he agrees, and smiles.

It isn't often I know something Jimmy doesn't. I try not to act all superior about it but I'm thinking that despite the odd total screw-up, I may be onto a good thing with this German-speaking. I'll just have to learn more words. I'll admit it, I'm glad I have him as a Freund. And I'm sehr glad Jemmy has him.

Show Time

SATURDAY MORNING I'M up before the sun, at the barn getting Peony ready. If you think that's crazy for Lisa on a Saturday, High Five to you, but keep in mind it's October, sunrise isn't until seven-thirty, and it takes an hour to braid Peony's mane even though I've been vigilant about keeping it thinned and short. Peony is standing patiently in the crossties while I'm up on the stool I brought from the pantry, fussing with the braids that didn't turn out well in hopes of getting them as neat and tight as the ones Bailey does, with limited success.

I got my grooming tote and all my tack cleaned, organized and ready to go last night. This morning, I have my jacket on a hanger in a garment bag ready to go into the truck, and I'm wearing my breeches under my sweats. Whoever thought up riding horses in white pants and black jackets was on the wrong track as I'm sure you'll agree it should be the other way around, if you need the white at all.

This is one area western has it over dressage. Have you seen the beautiful things the girls showing in Western Pleasure wear? Bright colours and rhinestone this and that! No white pants there! By comparison, a bunch of dressage riders look really boring, everyone dressed in penguin suits, hard to even tell them apart. Still, it looks classy and makes me feel like I'm a member of an elite club, you know, with uniforms.

Even with what I bought at the tack shop, I'm still borrowing stuff from Bailey. She's letting me wear this most gorgeous stock with embroidery and crystals on the part that's supposed to look like a knot, and a hair net with crystals on it, too. It's not the kind of hairnet you're thinking of that you have to wear in food prep that covers your whole head and makes you look like the old charwoman in *The Charwoman's Shadow*, who I'm sure you know is really a beautiful young girl who has had a magic spell put on her. Bailey's hairnet is just a sort of bag to put your bun in.

Trying to get my hair into any kind of bun will be a challenge and will require many bobby pins, though, owing to the fact I cut it off last spring and it hasn't grown out enough. Bailey says she'll help. She'll have time, because her rides aren't until the afternoon, whereas mine are first thing.

Going early in the morning has its benefits, a big one being there is almost no one around to watch. The big crowds show up around the middle of the day, Bailey says. But by big crowds, she means a couple dozen people, fifty tops. A dressage show isn't a great draw as spectator sports go, not in Nanaimo, anyway. Still, a lot of the contestants are around and maybe that's worse because they know what they're looking at and will notice if you screw up.

A couple of days ago, Trent texted me to ask if I had my ride times, and I texted back: nine fifteen and nine forty-five. He replied with a thumbs up emoji. I'm not sure what that means. Good luck, I guess. I don't expect to see him here because no one in their right mind would show up at that time of the morning just to watch someone they barely know ride for eight minutes.

If you're wondering, I haven't seen Trent since Monday. Between his job and mine, and homework and getting ready for the show, there just hasn't been time, so all we've done is exchange texts. He put a video one of his friends took of him "making friends with the mud" on Facebook, but he doesn't post much so it's not like I can stalk him there. I don't go on Facebook much, anyway, maybe just a few minutes here and there, and I don't watch the videos, unless they start by themselves and are very short. It just seems like a waste of time, plus sometimes people say things that are mean, which I can do without.

In that vein, remember I mentioned posting a photo of Peony in her new bridle? And all the nice comments except for that one mean one? Well, although I posted it weeks ago, last night there was a new comment. Another person I don't even know wrote: *A big ugly horse for a big ugly girl.* The only person I told about it was Jimmy. He looked up the person who made the comment and told me it was a troll which he figured out because it was a new page and had no friends, and blocked him or her for me. He looked at my privacy settings and said whoever it was shouldn't have been able to see the post because I made it so only friends or friends of friends could see it. Which I guess means that troll is a friend of a friend. So from now on when I post something, it will be for friends only.

If I thought last year's bullying was over just because it was a new school year, I was fooling myself. There may not be any hip-checking or pushing down, but there are other ways to bully someone if you really want to, thanks to social media.

I look at Peony patiently watching everything I do. I imagine there is adoration in her one big, soft, brown eye. I've brushed her so much she's positively gleaming and braided for the show, she looks regal, in my opinion. I feel a tug of affection. Even her missing eye makes her beautiful or at least makes me love her more.

How could anyone say Peony, beautiful inside and out, is ugly? I know I shouldn't let it bother me, but I can't stop thinking about it. Now, when my stomach is already squeezing with nerves about the show, is about the worst time. I push it out of my mind and focus on checking and re-checking everything. I'm ready and waiting.

I don't have to ride up to Elke's because Marci and Bailey are going to swing by and pick us up here at seven-thirty. They will already have Bailey's horse, Chip, in the trailer so Peony shouldn't be afraid to go in. I know she came to the rescue in a trailer and was trailered from the rescue to here, but that was months ago. We're apprehensive she might not want to go in so it might take a while. We've given ourselves plenty of time.

As it turns out, it's more time than we need because Peony just sniffs at the floor of the trailer for a moment before walking right in. Bailey flips the lead rope up over Peony's back as she goes by and quickly latches the butt bar behind her, then closes the door. I'm in the little area at the front, behind the panel that prevents a horse from going further in, and all I have to do is snap the trailer tie onto Peony's halter and remove the lead. I go out through the tack room, make sure all the doors are securely latched, and go to the passenger door of the truck. With Peony loaded no trouble I relax a bit.

"Well, that was easy," Bailey comments as we climb into the truck. She's small, so she's relegated to the half-size seat in the back, while I get the nice bucket seat in front. Just one more instance of long legs working to my advantage!

Marci climbs into the driver's seat, buckles her seatbelt, starts the engine and we pull away. "Peony is such a good girl," she says as she pulls up to the stop sign at the end of our road and checks for traffic before heading out. "At some point, someone taught her to load."

"Must have, I guess. Hard to imagine training her like that, and then just throwing her away."

"Oh, that's right, she's a rescue," Marci says. After a moment, she adds, "She's lucky to have you."

"I'm lucky to have her." I ruminate for a minute or two, then blurt out, "Do you think she's ugly? I mean, honestly? Maybe because of her eye?" I know, saying that makes me sound like I'm ten, and I must be a small person to fish for a compliment.

Marci and Bailey both exclaim at once, "No, my god no!" and so on. Then Bailey says, "She's stunning, Lisa! Where do you get that idea? And she has movement to die for! We need to video you sometime so you can see for yourself."

"Oh, I, umm, someone on Facebook said she's ugly."

"Well I would unfriend that person right away! And while you're at it, block her!" Bailey exclaims. "What kind of a *despicable* person would even make a comment like that?"

"Lisa," Marci says, "Bailey is right. Put it out of your mind. Only a vile person would make a mean-spirited comment like that. When you go into the ring this morning, don't even think about it. Think about how good you and Peony look, and remember that you're doing something very cool."

"Mom's right," Bailey says.

Okay, so the people that count, meaning Top Shelf Horse People, don't think Peony is ugly. I'm glad I didn't repeat the entire comment. I may not be above fishing for compliments for Peony but telling them the entire comment would be fishing for a compliment for myself. I'm not going to put anyone on the spot and I wouldn't believe anyone if they told me I was pretty anyway. I'm just happy Marci and Bailey, and of course Elke, like Peony.

It's a good thing Peony didn't give us any trouble getting into the trailer, because there is a crew working on replacing a utility pole that someone must have crashed into. Traffic is down to one lane alternating, which adds ten minutes to the trip.

When we get to the show grounds, Bailey and I go in search of our stall assignments and the exhibitor package from the show committee (our number, program and so on), and then Marci parks the truck and trailer. We offload the horses, Chip first. Peony lets out a huge whinny and dances around a bit. I clip her lead rope on, then release the trailer tie and Marci unlatches the butt chain. I ask Peony to go back, and she carefully steps out, with Marci catching her lead rope as she does. Good thing she's quick because Peony promptly does her giraffe imitation. You have no idea how high a seventeen-two hand horse can put its head! Her ears are pricked up; she dances around and bellows out another whinny.

Marci laughs. "I think Chip is her new best friend," she says. "It's amazing how attached they can get during even a short trailer ride."

She hands me the lead rope and I lead Peony into the stall next to Chip. She gives the stall a good sniffing all over and in minutes is back to her usual quiet self. We have to tack up and get to the warm-up ring right away, because I'll be called into the ring in half an hour. Half an hour! I think I'm going to throw up.

Alexis and Samantha (from the rescue, remember?) show up as I'm trying to coax my hair into a bun. They stopped at Tim Horton's on their way here and have coffee for everyone, plus the fifty-piece size box of TimBits. Normally I'd be all over both the coffee and the little donut pieces but with my stomach doing somersaults, I pass on both. They put their offerings on the fender of the trailer and take over my hair predicament. With only about five hundred grams of bobby pins, the little bun is firmly in place.

Bailey is calmly eating TimBits and drinking coffee, chit-chatting about this and that while Marci does most of the tacking up. I focus on getting myself organized, taking my sweats off, finding my jacket.

Marci gets Alexis to pin my number to my saddle pad. Then Marci hands me the reins; I lead Peony to one of the mounting blocks and get my sehr goot rider's body into the saddle.

Marci is walking along beside us, too, and bemoans the fact I have to ride first, because it would have been nice for me to be able to watch a few other riders, if only to see what they do while waiting for the bell, what they do at the end and so on. I'm not worried because Bailey has given me instructions about five hundred times, and that's just this morning.

Bailey follows with a cloth and wipes my boots which from a distance might actually look shiny, then we're off to the warm-up ring. Although I'm the first rider in today's show, there are a few others already warming up.

One horse is acting up, leaping and rearing. The rider just gets going again, when the horse sets off bucking some more. This time the rider goes off and the horse races around the ring, still bucking here and there. Peony gets all juiced up watching that and feels like a coiled spring under me. She's got the giraffe thing going on again. Forget about being on the bit! She bobbles around. If my nerves were bad before, this does nothing to settle them.

"Get out, Lisa," Bailey calls out, and opens the gate just wide enough for me. Fortunately I'm not far from the gate, and out we go. She closes the gate just as the loose horse runs toward it, maybe thinking to escape. Finding it blocked, he spins and gallops off the other way.

The fallen rider is up, apparently unhurt, and several people go into the ring to try and catch the horse. This takes a few minutes. It's a big ring and a horse that doesn't want to be caught can keep everyone running around for a while. Finally it's cornered and gives up, but by this time, the whipper-in is at the gate looking for me.

Elke, with Dixie on a leash, appears next to us as we're heading back to the show ring. "Goot morning, everyone!" she says cheerily. "Sorry I didn't get here sooner. Dixie run off unt I had a hard time to catch her. Are you all set, Lisa?"

"She didn't get a warm-up," Marci tells her. "There was some drama in the warm-up ring."

"Oh, zat's too bad! Vell, Lisa, you can go into zuh show ring now, unt varm up as best you can around zuh outside. Practice a couple canter departs. I don't see zuh judge in zuh stand yet so you vill haff some time. Use zuh corners! Let Peony see everysing. When zuh bell rings, you haff forty-five seconds to start. Zat's plenty of time, don't rush! Unt remember to smile! You unt Peony look great unt you vill do fine!"

So I go through the gate with Bailey at my side. (Being my caller, she's allowed.) I ride around the outside of the white board surround.

The surround is only about a foot high and I wonder if I'll be able to keep Peony inside of it. There are meter-high white pylons marking the letters that could be hiding gremlins. Peony gives everything a good look but seems to be back to her normal, calm self, taking it all in stride. I ask her to trot and then ride deep into the corner and ask for canter. Just a few strides, then back to trot. I have time to do this a couple times each way.

Bailey stands quietly just outside the surround at B. Before I know it, there are two people in the judging stand, the bell rings, and Bailey calls out, "A. Enter working trot. X. Halt. Salute. Proceed working trot!"

I head for A at trot, making sure I have her bent around my inside leg and she's firmly on the bit, careful not to overshoot the centerline as I turn in.

It's hard to believe four minutes can be so long! I'm very glad to have Bailey calling the test for me, because although I thought I knew it, there are moments when my brain just goes blank. The left lead canter is the third movement, thankfully early in the test, and Peony picks it up no problem. What a relief to have that behind us!

We have a bobble where I pick up the reins after the free walk, and we're a bit late picking up right lead canter, but no major problems. Everything goes well until the final salute. I release the reins and nudge Peony forward toward the judge as Bailey explained I should do before turning away, when it's as if Peony just noticed there was something inside the booth. In the blink of an eye, she spins and heads for the gate at a dead run. I barely cling to the saddle after that spin, but thankfully, manage to haul her to a stop in a most unsubtle, un-dressage-riderish way. When my heart stops pounding I realize I'm mortified.

Marci and Elke are waiting for me as I exit the ring, and Bailey follows me out. I almost don't want to see anyone, I'm so unhappy about that spook and how badly I rode it. But Elke says, "Goot ride, Lisa!"

"Oh...that spook! Why did I have her on a loose rein?"

"But you *should* giff her a loose rein ven you finish your test! Zat's her reward! Unt besides, vut spook?" Elke asks with a smile, and pats Peony's shoulder. I know for sure she saw it. Everyone did. Who could miss seeing me practically hanging off Peony's side? It's her "didn't happen" approach to spooks and blunders. "You rode vell. Now ve go to zuh warm-up ring unt do a little somesing for a few minutes. You haff only maybe twenty minutes before your next ride! Put ziss on. I help you." She hands me the earpiece, picks Dixie up and marches off toward the warm up ring, Marci, Bailey, Alexis, Samantha, Peony and me in tow.

"You did great," Bailey assures me as she walks along beside me.

"I'm so glad you were calling for me, Bailey! My mind went into neutral. I'd've been lost without you!"

"It gets easier with practice," she tells me.

"You rode it accurately," Marci chips in. "You can do even better in Test Two now that you know you need to ask for right lead canter a little sooner. Or try a little stronger aid."

I nod. That makes sense. And then I'm in the warm-up ring away from everyone else, no wild runaway horses this time, with Elke coaching me. I hear the announcer and the caller for the rider in the show ring and notice the dust from a small whirlwind passing along the fence, but these things are just background as I focus on what Elke is telling me. It's calming, for both me and Peony. In minutes, the whipper-in is looking for me and off we go for our second test.

I'm riding around the outside of the surround waiting for the bell when I see Trent standing with Marci and Elke. He smiles as I go by. OMG this is the last thing I needed to see seconds before my test! As if sensing my jolt of nerves, Peony suddenly thinks the marker pylon at F is the scariest thing she's seen in her life and where is her BFF Chip when she needs him? I feel her body, tense and quivering beneath me, as she bellows out a huge whinny. If the judge rings the bell now, I don't think I can even get her to halt at X!

But she must be busy with writing remarks on the previous ride or she's the kindest judge in the world, as the bell doesn't go until Peony gives up her fire breathing dragon impersonation. We get a nice square halt at X and off we go.

You might think all I have to do is make sure I get the right lead canter depart on time, and my second test will be better than the first, but you can forget about it! This time, Peony takes right lead when I ask for left. I'm glad I practiced fixing it, but the damage is done. I'm so apprehensive about the free walk, which in this test is on a shallow loop instead of across the diagonal, she jogs. This is doubly bad because the movement has a coefficient of two. I'm so glad when the test is over I could almost cry. And then the judge stands and motions me toward her. I didn't know this could happen.

"Good morning!" she says when I'm standing in front of her.

"Good morning," I reply. If I wasn't sweating before, I am now. Did I do something wrong?

"Your mare—what is her breeding?"

"I, er, don't know. She was a rescue."

"A rescue! Well, lucky you! She's lovely and you make a good pair. Keep up the good work."

I nod. I feel so happy I think I could cry and I worry I might have a cry face. I press my lips together and can't speak, not even to thank her, but she's sitting down again, discussing something with the scribe. I'm dismissed. The next rider is going around the outside of the surround as I make my way to the exit gate.

Elke asks, "Goot job, Lisa!"

"Thank you," I say. I turn to Trent and manage to muster a smile. "Hi, Trent!"

"Good morning!" he says.

"What did the judge say?" Bailey wants to know. I tell them, and Elke says, "Sehr goot! Now ve put Peony away and help Bailey to get ready, ja?"

We all head for the barns. I dismount and run my stirrups up so I can walk beside Trent. After the others have gotten a bit ahead of us, I ask, "When did you get here?"

"In time to watch your first ride, if that's what you're asking," he says. "You were busy with your horse people so I waited until now to come over."

"Oh. So you saw the train wreck at the end."

"Man, Lisa! That spin and dig out was something else!"

"Yeah, uh, not fun."

"Didn't know Peony could move that fast!"

"Well, now that some riders have GPS tracking, they've found out a horse can spook at fifty KPH."

"What? Really? So the spook, that jump and spin, could be at fifty kilometers per hour?"

"They can't run that fast, you understand. Just the first jump or two."

"Thank god my bike can't go from zero to fifty that quick! You were great! I can't believe anyone could stay on! And recover to ride again a few minutes later."

"Really?"

"Really." He takes my free hand and pulls me to a stop. "I have to go to work. Wish I didn't, but I'm already late. See you later?"

I nod and say, "See you later."

He gives my hand a squeeze. His eyes are intense; so blue they're nearly purple. After a moment, he releases my hand, turns and heads through the people and horses, avoiding the occasional pile of horse dung, aiming for the parking lot.

BAILEY, AS I EXPECTED, did what I thought was a fine job on her only ride, but she was disappointed. She was worried about canter half pass and it went fine, but her three flying changes that were supposed to happen on the diagonal with four strides between each, didn't. One had five, one had two, and Chip threw in an extra one, requiring another change to get on the correct lead for the left turn at E. I don't know how many times she came up with various reasons for the extra lead change. To her credit, not once did she blame Chip.

This is my first time at a dressage show, so I'm not sure how everything works and don't know how to find out what the judge and scribe were busy writing down. Turns out they post the results on a bulletin board and you can pick up your test, and your ribbon if you're lucky enough, on a table just outside the show office.

I find the Training Level Test One list and start at the bottom. Twelve people rode this test. If you think I'm surprised to see my name at the top of the list, and my test on the table with a red ribbon stapled to it, High Five to you! In fact, shocked would be more accurate, if there is such a thing as Happy Shocked. My score: sixty-five percent! The judge's remarks at the bottom: "Very well organized and harmonious ride. A pleasure to watch." I nearly did my Peony Feel Good Buck! This is the happiest I've ever been to get sixty-five percent on a test. Well, I'd be ecstatic to get it on a chem test because so far I'm lucky to get fifty. But I'm not thinking about that, what with the bliss of seeing my name at the top of the list!

You're probably thinking, sixty-five percent and that's the best of the twelve tests? I should point out my score was only a fraction of a percentage point better than the next one so it's not like Peony and I were, like, Stand-Out Stars and people will be wanting my autograph and photos of me with her anytime soon. One extra bobble and we could've been at the bottom of the list.

Marci says dressage is a sport for perfectionists. Bailey says it's a sport for the anal retentive. I'm sure you know me well enough by now to realize if I'm either of those, it's the latter.

And what happened in Test Two? It's a little more difficult than Test One as I mentioned, with the free walk loop, but you still have from one letter through the corner to the next to get your canter depart. I got right lead canter where it was supposed to be, but apparently some of our circles had corners on them, one trot circle wasn't big enough, and Peony was counter-flexed to gawk at the people who weren't in the stand for our first test. I have to admit I wasn't prepared for it and got distracted, too. I let Peony turn her whole head and it's a pretty big head so no one could miss it, even from the far end of the arena where the judge sits. The result? The test wasn't better, it was ten percentage points lower, and no ribbon there. I don't care, really. Nothing could top this red ribbon!

And then I realize the ribbon was just the cherry on top of the sundae. It would have been an awesome day without it. All my new friends helping me so much, Trent showing up even if only for a few minutes and squeezing my hand, but most of all, my wonderful Peony being such a star, spook aside because that didn't happen as you know, on her first time ever at a show.

Nikki and Trevor

"TREVOR! TREVOR!"

He hears her calling. She's looking for him. Again. *My god,* he thinks, *she's like a heat-seeking missile! You'd think she'd figure out that if I wanted to see her, she wouldn't have to come looking for me.*

He puts down the wrench, gets to his feet and goes to the garage door where he stands and watches her coming toward him.

When she sees him, she begins swinging her hips provocatively, and smiles. He can't deny she's attractive: curves in all the right places, pretty face, the whole package.

"Well, there you are," she says as she draws near. "What are you doing? You haven't answered my texts."

"I, uhh, well. Working on my bike. I have to get this done. Bad enough I had to work all day so..."

"Well," she interrupts, "don't you know all work and no play is Just! No! Good!" She punctuates this with playful punches to his bicep. "You're only young once! Come on, Trev, it's Saturday night! A bunch of us are going to the river. Go get changed!"

"Nikki, no. I'm in the middle of something here. I want to get this done so I can ride tomorrow."

"Oh what's so important about riding tomorrow, when you could come to the river with me tonight? I'm bringing a sleeping bag. It cools down after dark, you know."

He studies her face, then her body. He has to admit the display in the bikini top is enticing. Maybe he can finish up the repair on his dirt bike first thing in the morning and still get to the track in time to ride. It's tempting. Very.

"Give me half an hour," he says, and flicks the switch next to the door to turn off the garage lights.

HE'S WEARING HIS GREEN polo shirt with the Incredible Edibles logo, ready to leave for work, when he sees Nikki's car pull in next to his in the driveway. She gets out, looks up at the window where he's standing, and waves. He lifts a hand in acknowledgement.

They've been having some steaming hot sessions, and she's an amazing girl, but he feels a twinge of irritation at her showing up everywhere he goes, even today, even though he texted her that he has to work. He grabs his backpack, sets the alarm and goes out the door to meet her.

"Hey, Nikki, I told you I have to work today."

"I know, *silly*, I'm not *stupid*! You said your dad was away. I thought we might have a little time alone."

"Too late, Nikki."

"Okay, well then, at least I can give you a goodbye kiss." She slides up to him, puts her arms up around his shoulders and presses herself against him, kissing his neck, then his mouth.

So much girl pressed against him like this stirs a response, but today, running late, he really doesn't have time. He takes her forearms in his hands and pulls them off. Holding her hands, he plants a peck on her lips, then drops her hands and steps away, opening his car door. "I gotta go. See you later," he says, and slides into the driver's seat.

"That's all the thanks I get for going to the trouble to come over here? For thinking of you?" Her face isn't pretty when it's twisted into a pout; much worse when she's scowling like now. It's something he's seen a few times already, although they've only been going together for a month.

He wonders what she expected. It's not like they're married or even going steady. They just get together for a good time now and then. Well, he has to admit it's been pretty steady. Several times a week. Still. It wasn't supposed to be a commitment, just fun and games. That's what she said at the beginning, and he took her at her word.

He rolls down the window and says, "Thanks. See you later." He musters a smile and drives away. Out on the frontage road he checks his look in the mirror and digs through the glove box for a Kleenex to get rid of the lipstick. Besides the smears on his skin, there's a smudge on his collar, but luckily it hardly shows.

He pulls up to the stop sign at the main road and as he waits for traffic to clear, looks out at the acreage on the corner. Unlike his place, this property has been cleared and is mostly grass with just a few tall native firs. At the far end of the driveway, past the house and garage, is the barn. There's often a horse nearby. Today, there's a girl just climbing onto the horse. He's seen her riding along the road a few times, but he's never met her. He'd watch for a bit longer, whether or not he was running late, but Nikki's car pulls up behind him. He pulls out onto the road heading south and is relieved when Nikki's car turns the other way.

HE CONGRATULATES HIMSELF on meeting the horse girl, Arielle, even if it meant pretending interest in the horse farm at the end of the road. Now he's walking along the road beside her. It's sort of a date, they arranged ahead of time for him to go with her. She's riding a huge horse and he has to hustle to keep pace. He's prattled on like a fool, telling her all about himself. Even about his parents. But she's easy to talk to, asking him about everything, commenting how nice it is he's made friends even though he's only lived here a short while.

The subject of friends is a bit of a sticky point. Nikki has said a few things about Arielle, so he knows they're acquainted. Would it be a mistake to mention Nikki at all? What will he say if she asks him if Nikki is his girlfriend? He screws up his courage and asks, "Hey, do you know the girl who lives across the road from me? Nikki?"

"Yeah, sure," Arielle says. She gives him an unreadable look before going on to say, "We've been friends since grade eight. She's very pretty."

"Yeah." It's all he can think of to say. What else is there? He can't say what he's thinking, namely that Nikki only talks about Arielle when it's to make fun of her big feet or flat chest or creepy friends. He realizes that says more about Nikki than Arielle and decides he'd like to see more of Arielle. She's told him about the horse show on the weekend. His class and work schedules have him booked up this week, and Nikki has been nagging him about a movie. She can be very demanding. He will just have to find a way to work it out.

AND WORK IT OUT, HE does. All week, he made excuses not to see Nikki. Even so, she showed up in the garage on Wednesday and complained his bike didn't look any different; he wasn't really working on it, just wasting time; it was a lousy excuse for not taking her to a movie and so on. She ended up screaming at him, something about how if he thought he was going to get laid anytime soon, he had another thing coming. She stormed out the door and drove away, spewing gravel.

Thinking about it since, he wonders if he might regret it. Then he realizes he can easily get back into her good graces if he wants to. More likely it's time to move on, even if it's not with Arielle.

Saturday morning before work, he goes to watch Arielle ride in the horse show. He's there in time to witness her horse make a crazy wild maneuver and yet somehow, she stays on, stops the horse and calmly rides on.

He walks with her friends back to the stable and when she gets off to walk beside him, he takes her hand. It feels natural. She's tall and slim; the word *willowy* pops into his head and he realizes it describes her perfectly. Her face is flushed with exertion and the excitement of the show and he's struck by how alluring she is. "I can't stay," he says, "But I'll see you later?"

"See you later," she agrees.

When their eyes meet, he feels a tug of desire and wants to kiss her. Would she object? He doesn't think so, but a first kiss here? With all the horses and people milling around? Instead, he gives her hand a squeeze and leaves before he can make a fool of himself.

On his break later, he texts her to ask if she would like to go for a Frosty after work. She says it's too cool for a Frosty but agrees to go with him anyway.

HE DRIVES TO THE PARKING lot at Waterfront Plaza and they walk along the seawall. It's a beautiful evening, although with the sun dipping low in the sky, much of the wide walkway is in the shade. They stop outside the ice cream shop. He says, "Hey, not a Frosty, but how about a waffle cone?"

"I thought we agreed it's not ice cream weather," she says.

"You said it wasn't. I just didn't argue."

She laughs but goes along with it and he buys two waffle cones. They chat amiably as they stroll along, licking their ice cream as they go. When they cross the bridge into the park, he pulls her down beside him on the first bench they come to and they sit, watching the boats bobbing quietly at their moorage. There are a couple of teenagers down on the sand by the lagoon, skipping stones across the still face of the water, and couples stop on the bridge to look across the channel to the houses on Protection Island, their windows gilded by the setting sun.

When she finishes her cone, Arielle says, "Thank you. That was good! Okay ice cream weather after all."

"I told you! And you're welcome."

"Such a beautiful evening," she says with a sigh.

"Not as beautiful as you."

"Oh!" she says, her eyes widening.

The last bit of sunlight ignites the red tones in her hair for just a second. He leans in, pulls her close and kisses her.

OKAY, I KNOW, IT'S obvious who this story is about and this is without a doubt the sappiest thing I've ever written. Why did I do it? Because if I can write someone out of my life, maybe I can write someone in.

Real Life

IF YOU'RE WONDERING why there was no parent at the show to witness my Debut Performance, it's because Jemmy had a karate tournament in Victoria. Although Dad assured us he would still take Jemmy to karate, he couldn't make it. He was too busy getting settled into his new place to take a whole Saturday going to Victoria, you know how bad the traffic is, it can take an hour just to get from downtown to Goldstream Park and then there's the Malahat stretch of the highway which is always a nightmare, and so on. Jemmy was disappointed and Mom was fuming.

The Victoria Traffic Excuse wouldn't fly as a reason for not coming to watch me ride, but I hadn't told Dad about the show so it saved me having to pretend to accept some other flimsy excuse. Besides, there was the possibility he'd show up with his girlfriend and I am SO not ready for that.

At least he let us know the night before. Mom didn't say much, other than muttering something about how she has other things to do on her day off too. It was obvious she was going to be cranky for a while. No one could miss the slamming of cupboard doors as she put dishes away.

I remember seeing this performance many times when she was mad at Dad. At least I think it was Dad she was mad at this time and not me, even though I hadn't gotten around to emptying the dishwasher. I suggested the dishes would be fine left in the dishwasher until we needed them, something I've argued for in the past. Mom didn't agree. I think she just needed something to vent about until her temper cooled. Man, is she ever fast at sorting the cutlery into the drawer!

Watching her storm around, it struck me that the divorce could have been Mom's fault. She does have a temper, something she says is normal for redheads. How many times did Dad ask what was wrong and she just pressed her lips into a hard line and went around slamming cupboard doors but wouldn't answer? And then there's the fact that if she used the BMW, she wouldn't put gas in it even if the gauge should slip below a quarter of a tank. She didn't do his laundry, either, because she says he's too fussy about things that can't go in the dryer. He ended up hanging everything over the railings around the loft, which was another thing Mom bitched at him about. And would it have killed her to buy meat for him when she's already at the store?

Well, anyway. When she was done slamming cupboard doors I assured her it was okay not to come to the show because it didn't make sense for Jemmy to miss his tournament just to watch me ride for a total of eight minutes. Also there would be lots of other shows.

Jimmy would have come, but he was booked in at McDonald's and not only that, it's a long way from the Northgate to the show grounds on a bicycle. These were not feeble excuses. He really wanted to go because he loves Peony almost as much as I do and he's a great groom.

Because Mom still seems a little put out about the whole Dad not taking Jemmy to Victoria thing and possibly also our discussion about the pros and cons of leaving the dishes in the dishwasher, on Sunday without even being asked I spend hours doing housework: vacuuming, dusting, and even cleaning all the toilets not just the one by the back door.

Then I go out to the shed and start the lawnmower, meaning to tackle at least the area in front of the house. With Dad gone, it's gotten quite long but it's late in the season so it will be the last mowing of the year. Who knows, by spring Dad might be back so I'll never have to do it again. Meanwhile, lots of Brownie Points, right? But although I manage to drive it around, quite expertly in my opinion, I can't make it actually mow. I figure it must be related to the red knob but pushing and jiggling it does nothing.

Jimmy shows up when I'm making my third trip around the yard. When I stop next to him, he says "You're not cutting anything."

"Duh!" I say.

"Why not?"

I explain at length about the red knob, my attempts at getting it to do something, and what use is it anyway? I'll admit to using some words I'd rather not repeat here, and maybe I'm a little loud, I'm that frustrated. Maybe there's more of Mom in me than just the big feet and small boobs. Jimmy seems to think it's amusing, which is no help.

"So...Do you think if you keep driving around it will somehow magically start mowing?"

"I'm not *that* stupid!" I exclaim, and give him my best stink eye. He's lucky there's no empty beer can in the cup holder or I would have thrown it at him. Maybe I would have thrown one that wasn't empty.

He laughs, which may be a sign he disagrees. It doesn't make him my favourite person at the moment. Then he says, "Go on, Lisa. I'll do it."

I climb off before he can change his mind. Mom must have been watching, because just as Jimmy is settling into the seat, she comes out and hands him a bottle of his favourite kombucha. It fits nicely into the drink holder. I think she spoils him. You know how expensive those things are? She didn't bring me a drink, not even a cheapie Pepsi which I hardly ever drink because I don't like fizzy stuff but that's not the point. Of course, she's probably thinking Jimmy must be thirsty after riding his bike here.

"Thanks, Mrs. Rogney!" he says. He pulls the red knob up, the mower starts whirring, and away he goes.

"I think he should come and live with us," Mom says as we watch him drive away, leaving a swath of neatly-mown lawn and the scent of cut grass in his wake. Before I can say anything, she turns and goes into the house without asking my opinion of that idea, so she can't see the surprise on my face. I never thought it was a possibility. How could it happen? Does it take a while to be approved as foster parents? Could Mom be a Foster Mom without a Foster Dad? I'll look into it.

While I'm on the computer looking at the government site regarding foster parenting, I make the mistake of opening my Facebook page and before I know it, I'm posting the photo Bailey texted me of a surprisingly good moment in one of our tests. I add a boast about the red ribbon. I get a Like one of my Saskatchewan cousins almost right away.

It's nearing dinner time. I go down to see if I can peel potatoes. As you know, it's about the only thing I'm good at, cooking-wise, aside from the vegan chili I mentioned earlier and anyway, I want to tell Mom what I found out about foster parenting from the government website.

MONDAY, I'M ON MY WAY to the lunchroom when I hear barking and I'm surrounded by The Coven. Nicole and Laurie Ann scurry up so they're right in front of me, blocking my way.

"You better leave my boyfriend alone, bitch!" Nicole hisses at me.

If looks could kill! Even so much smaller than me, she's downright intimidating. I muster all my courage and ask, "How did you get a boyfriend with that STD, Nicole?"

She sputters for a second before telling the world: "I don't have an STD and I never did have an STD!"

Her defensive reaction is empowering. I say, "Not so loud! Everyone heard you!"

She looks around, notices the kids who seem to be listening, and lowers her voice. "I mean it," she hisses, "if you don't stay away from him, you'll be sorry."

"I would leave him alone, if I knew who you meant..."

"You know who I mean! Trent! Leave him alone, or you'll be sorry. And if you think that ugly horse of yours is beautiful, you must mean only when compared to *you*."

"Yeah," Laurie Ann pipes up, "You're ugly! How can you stand being so ugly?"

"How can you stand being so tall?" Haggedy asks.

"Why don't you just kill yourself?" Broom Hilda asks, and Haggedy and the other members of The Coven crow as if it's the funniest thing they've heard in their lives.

"Leave Trent alone!" Haggedy advises, "or you'll be sorry!"

The Witches of Westview Secondary are still cackling as they move off, assimilated into the mob of kids heading for the lunchroom. Although I think I held up my end well, certainly better than usual, I decide I'll avoid the possibility of further exposure to The Coven and eat my lunch outside today. Jimmy will have to content himself with the other Untouchables. If Maureen's there, he won't mind.

Once outside, I find a spot on the retaining wall, and sit. I eat my all-time most favourite sandwich, peanut butter with bread and butter pickles on multigrain, in a hurry, because the concrete is too cold to sit on for long.

I don't understand why Nicole feels she has to warn me to stay away from Trent. It's not like we've had any actual dates. Even though I fantasized about it, there was no text after the horse show, no walk along the seawall, no romantic kiss on the park bench. And furthermore, it's not like I'm chasing him! He's the one who's initiated everything.

And why the comment about Peony? We're not Facebook friends anymore, and anyway, when I posted about the show, I didn't say Peony was beautiful. Then it occurs to me: in a text exchange with Trent, I said something about my beautiful horse and how I was so proud of her at the show. Did he show that to Nicole? Is that what she's picked about, me texting him?

Maybe there's no amount of writing stories with happy endings that will change real life.

Eighteen

WITH ALL THE FOCUS on the horse show, my birthday wasn't front of mind and kind of snuck up on me. The night before, Mom told me she was going to get a cake, and suggested I invite Bailey and Angie. Jimmy, of course, is a given. It wouldn't be a big soirée. It is a school night after all. I sent a text invitation to Bailey and Angie. Bailey accepts immediately. Angie texts back: "Sorry can't. Movie with Jarrett."

I told everyone I didn't want a present, just the pleasure of their company and help eating a Black Forest cake. Even so, there are gifts. Bailey gives me a beautiful hair net, black with a bunch of crystals and a little bow on it, so at future shows I don't have to borrow hers.

Jimmy got me a pair of earrings, little silver horseshoes with tiny diamonds. I hug him and kiss him and put them on right away, that's how much I like them.

Jemmy got me a pack of printer paper, which may not sound like much of a gift but he got it with his own allowance and it's very practical since I go through a lot of it. I give him a quick hug but no kisses, keeping in mind his girl-germ phobia.

My gift from Mom is a card. This surprises me because you may remember I was expecting the step-counting watch. Inside the card are five one hundred-dollar bills. There's the picture of the saddle Mom had taken down off her mirror, and the card is signed by both Mom and Dad. I'm so surprised and happy I could cry, for two reasons: one, I'll have my own saddle now; and two, Mom and Dad did this together? If they can collaborate on my gift, maybe they'll reconcile!

Mom interrupts my thoughts by announcing that I'm now two years overdue for getting my DL. I agree of course but don't know that she has to make it public like that. I guess everyone already knew anyway.

"Starting this week-end, we'll make a point of driving at least an hour every week," she says, "no excuses."

"When you get your license you can take me to karate!" Jemmy points out.

"That's right!" I realize that will help Mom out when Dad can't make it. It also dawns on me it's about time I quit making excuses and helped more. Is being eighteen different than being seventeen?

Mom has always said I'm a late bloomer. Maybe I have finally started to bloom. Or as Dad would say, Grow Up.

Fall Guy

I'VE JUST LEFT JIMMY and I'm on my way down the stairs to my locker to get ready for morning classes, when I see Broom Hilda, Haggedy and Laurie Ann, three abreast, coming up. They're not in a hurry, sauntering along, blocking the stairway so everyone behind them is delayed and everyone coming down has to get out of their way. They're the Westview Secondary Royalty after all. I scrunch as close to the wall as I can and get a good hold on the handrail.

Haggedy spots me and in a booming voice says, "Hey, look! It's Lesbo!"

They all give a couple of dog-barks, and then Broom Hilda calls out, "Hey, Lesbo! You're such a waste of oxygen you should do the world a favour and kill yourself!"

I keep looking straight ahead.

If anyone's a lesbian, I'd say it's Broom Hilda, makeup and jewelry and multi-coloured hair or not. Maybe that's all window dressing. If she is lesbian, which I don't know but if she is, she could never come out because her friends wouldn't accept her and in fact they'd make fun of her like they do me, that much I know for sure. Sad, no? For a second I feel sorry for her.

Broom Hilda isn't as tall as I am but she's way sturdier, with muscular legs and arms. I've seen her on the basketball court in PE and thank my lucky stars we're not in the same class because she's always knocking people down. Only when the teacher's back is turned, of course. Already this year she's bumped me a couple of times when we pass in the hall, so you understand why I'm careful.

There's plenty of room for the three of them to pass, but when they're just about level with me, Broom Hilda crouches and then launches herself at me. I react by hopping down to the next stair; in that split second, I hear a sort of meaty thump. I think she must have hit the wall.

Almost at the same instant, a guy behind me makes the mistake of laughing. You can guess what happens next. You'll have to guess, because since it happened behind me I didn't see it. I only know whatever she did resulted in him stumbling into me. My knees buckle and I might fall but he's grabbed onto me and down we both go, with me right on top of him.

The Coven seems to think this is the funniest thing they've seen in their lives. They're howling with laughter. But they know better than to hang around; they scurry away, cackling as they go.

I scramble to my feet and the boy under me doesn't waste any time getting up, either. He says he's sorry, I say I'm sorry too. I know it wasn't my fault but I'm mortified. In the midst of my embarrassment I have time to notice he's bigger than me and I would say, hot! But I don't want to linger and gawk and make it worse so I beat feet away.

I feel like crying, not because I got hurt, which I didn't, but I suppose it's the shock. The worst of it is, The Coven has moved past verbal insults and is getting physical again, and that's a scary thought. I wasn't worrying about it for nothing, see? I know I promised to report it. Now I have to decide if I can. When it comes down to it, I'm afraid it might make it worse. Maybe I'll wait and see if it happens again.

At lunch time, I don't tell Jimmy or the others. It's something I would have told Jimmy and Angie about, and I would have told Jimmy, but he and Maureen have their heads together and I don't want to interfere in what looks like a budding romance.

The rest of the girls aren't really friends, not in the come-over-to-my-place category. I don't know much about them, other than the alopecia thing and what classes we have together. They're big into Job's Daughters whatever that is and their projects in sewing class. Today we're treated to an update from Connie about the quilt she and her aunt are making out of old blue jeans. Some of the squares are even overlaid with her grandmother's crocheted doilies which you have to agree is awesome as a tribute or lasting memorial or any number of other nouns and adjectives. Although I muster an "ooooh!" along with the others, you can see we don't have much in common. I'm stewing about what happened and how stupid I must have looked sitting on that guy but keep it to myself.

I'm leaving the lunchroom planning to check the library to see if any of the books I've been waiting for are back in when Angie falls in beside me. "Hey, Angie," I say.

"I heard you fell," she says. "Are you okay?"

I stop walking and have a good look at her. She's not only Jarrett-less but she's wearing her pre-Jarrett clothes. "Yeah, umm, I'm okay. What did you hear about it?"

"What I heard was that you tripped and knocked Zach DeLoitte down. *Zach DeLoitte!*"

"What's so special about Zach DeLoitte?"

"Oh, Lisa, you're impossible."

"Anyway, that's not exactly what happened. Hey, where's Jarrett?"

"Umm. I dunno."

"Isn't he at school today?"

"Probably." Her mouth turns down. Her lower lip trembles and her forehead creases in a frown. "We broke up."

"Oh. Sorry." Did that sound sincere? It wasn't. If she has a broken heart I guess I should be sorry, but I can't help being glad. It's on the tip of my tongue to say something negative about the whole Angie/Jarrett hook-up, remind her I never thought it was a good idea, it's been hardly more than a month, and so on. Then I stop myself. Things like that are best left unsaid in case they get back together again.

"Yeah. I caught him with some bleach blonde bee-yotch."

I guess stalking him paid dividends after all. I shrug and say again, "Sorry."

"It's okay. You were right about him. I couldn't see it."

Do I crow about it and welcome her back as my Best Friend? The crowing part, no. The Best Friend, maybe. Not right away, though.

"I know him, that's all." Before the Jarrett Criticisms lurking in my head come out of my mouth, I add, "I gotta run. See you."

I leave her standing there. Just a little payback. I know, I'm a very small person for enjoying that moment.

I'm in luck; the book I was waiting for has come back in, so I sign it out. I'm on my back to my locker to get my books for the afternoon's classes when I see the guy I sat on coming toward me. He's with a couple of other guys. They stop when they reach me, and the fall guy says, "Hey! Are you sure you're okay? You ran off before I had a chance to apologize."

This is surprising for two reasons: one, I already told him I was okay; and two, he and his buddies are hot. Also, they're not Untouchables. And he thinks he should apologize? I guess that's really three or four reasons, but you know, the semi-colon thing.

I do know who these guys are even if I don't know their names. They're kind of the Guy Chapter of Westview Secondary Royalty, but unlike the Girl Chapter (the Coven), I've never heard anything bad about them. Would you believe they volunteered at PetSmart on Cat and Kitten Adoption Day? The Nanaimo Daily Report posted it on Facebook. All I remember from the photo was about half a dozen guys in matching jackets each holding a kitten. I'll have to see if I can find that post again and have a better look.

"I, umm, yeah, I'm okay, a little shocked I guess. What about you? You were, er, on the bottom."

"Ha! I play rugby. A pretty little girl landing in my lap is like winning a prize!"

Pretty? Little? Me?

"You got good reflexes! That was a quick reaction to get outta the way."

"Oh, umm, thanks. But I was half expecting it."

"Oh yeah? Why?"

"Umm, well, it's just...well...they always do something."

"Oh? *They*?"

"Umm, er, well, it's all of them. Laurie Ann Reedy and her sycophants. Zelda isn't here this year, so now I guess Broom Hilda is the muscle. I call them The Coven." If you're wondering, yes, I'm babbling like an idiot and yes, I can feel my face turning pink. Or maybe by now, red.

"The Coven? Like witches?"

Again I'm nodding like a bobblehead. I'd like to say something brilliant but all I can think of is, "Yeah. Witches."

"Broom Hilda, eh?" Going from the looks on their faces, the guys don't think it's stupid; in fact they're chuckling.

"Hey, my name's Zach, and these guys are Tony and Nathan."

He's introducing himself and his buddies? I look up, so astonished all I do is say "Hi."

"Er," Zach says, "and what do we call you?"

Duh! Only a misfit with no social graces forgets to tell the other person their name during introductions! "Lisa," I say. "Call me Lisa."

"Hey, Lisa! I guess, what did you call her? Broom Hilda? Broom Hilda didn't like being laughed at. I shouldn't have laughed, maybe, because she did hurt herself. But it was funny, her trying to ram you into the wall, missing and hitting it head first herself."

"Oh, that's what happened."

"Yeah, poetic justice. She was really gonna nail you. She should try out for the women's rugby team."

"She might've busted her nose," Tony says. "I heard she was at the nurse's office because she got a nosebleed."

Although a nosebleed is no laughing matter, all three of them chuckle and I admit it, I join in.

"She shouldn't've tripped me. If I hadn't run into you, I might've gone the rest of the way to the bottom and someone could've really got hurt. That's nothing to fool around with. Who is she, anyway?"

"I, umm, I, er, I don't know her name. I just think of her as Broom Hilda."

"I suppose you can't report it to the principal if you don't know her name. And maybe you don't want to anyway?"

I shake my head and look at my feet again.

"Okay, well, think about it. You can report it on line if that's easier. It was an assault, and she shouldn't get away with it."

I look up, straight into his nice warm brown eyes.

Nathan says, "Zach, you really think Dvorak would do anything? Other than give her a talking to and maybe few detentions that she'd skip anyway? There are other ways."

The boys jabber quietly among themselves huddle-like. I think I've been dismissed, when Zach turns to me and says, "Hey, you know, I was thinking, since you already sat in my lap, we must know each other well enough to go for a coffee sometime."

I think I just felt my eyes pop out of my head, so I remind myself he said 'sometime' which means probably never. I need to play it cool. "Yeah, umm, I, er, sure." Brilliant, coming from an up-and-coming novelist, right?

"Great! How about Saturday?'

"Zach," Tony pipes up, "we're on the road this week-end, remember?"

"Oh yeah! Damn!" He scowls, puts his hands on his hips and takes a few steps around before coming back to me. "Lisa, I'm sorry, I completely forgot. Can we do something next week, then?"

"I guess."

"Okay!" They turn away and as they go, Zach calls out over his shoulder, "Glad you're okay!"

I watch them walk away. Tony is the slimmest and shortest of the three, but they're all fine young male specimens. Has the Boyfriend Pool become an actual Pool, or at least a Puddle?

I know what you're thinking, 'something next week' is vague and I shouldn't pin my hopes on it. Still, I now have first-hand experience of what romance writers call 'floating on a cloud', because that's what I'm doing as I go to my desk.

I have to admit I was depressed after the Staircase Incident, assuming the news would have travelled around the school and by lunch time everyone would be getting a chuckle out of it. The Lisa Rogney Grade Twelve Experience was on track to be more dismal than the Grade Eleven Experience. Instead, well, Zach. This is just another reminder you should never assume, because no one seems to think the Staircase Incident was funny.

I'm on my way to the school bus after class when I see The Coven in the crowd milling around on the sidewalk. A male voice calls out, "Hey, Broom Hilda! What happened to your face?"

Another male voice yells back, "I heard she crashed her broom!" Everyone within earshot laughs.

Today couldn't get any better.

MOM LETS ME DRIVE TO work on Saturday. We're pretty comfortable one-on-one now. I feel a little sheepish for avoiding her. Think about it: she and Dad were married for twenty years, almost half her life, and now she has to get used to being single again.

Maybe Mom and Dad are both to blame for the divorce but life goes on and we're always going to be family and of course, there's always the possibility they will get back together. We haven't discussed the reasons for the split and I'm happy to keep it that way. But today, alone together in the privacy of the car, she brings it up.

"Are you missing Dad, Lisa?"

"Er..." What do I say to that? I'm not. We've texted back and forth and there was that awkward dinner, plus I see him when he comes to pick up Jemmy to take him to karate. I don't miss him. Then it hits me: is she about to tell me he might be moving back in?

"Not really. But it would be okay with me if, you know, if you guys got back together."

"Oh."

I admit I'm surprised and maybe a little disappointed she doesn't dive right in saying he is coming home and things can get back to normal. But maybe it's still in the negotiation phase. I'm glad I got my point across so she knows I would welcome Dad back. I think that's the end of the conversation and my mind is on my driving and the story in my head when she continues, "Have you wondered why we split?"

"Er, umm, not really. I just figured it was because of a lot of little things and not one big thing."

"Well, you're partly right."

"Oh! Is it because of his friend?"

"Yes, the one he lives with now..."

"I don't want to meet her!" I blurt out. I surprise myself. I thought I'd be all grown up about it but apparently I'm just going to continue avoiding emotional encounters. Besides, what's the point of meeting her? He's going to have to dump her anyway.

I check the mirrors and do a shoulder check before changing lanes so I can get into the left turn bay ahead. Again I think that's the end of the topic. And once again, I'm wrong.

"We're not going to get back together, Lisa," she says. "What I want you to know, so you're prepared for it—so you can get used to the idea—he's not with another woman. He's with another man."

I'm still letting that sink in when I pull into the parking lot and stop near the doors.

"I hope you understand, Lisa. It wasn't easy for him. He loves us. That's why he stayed with us so long."

At that moment I realize the divorce is not his fault or her fault or the fault of both, because neither of them is to blame. My head is spinning.

There are cars behind us, so no time for discussion. All I can do as I shift into park is look at her before the guy behind me toots the horn. I guess if you're heading for the drive-through because you want food in a hurry, you don't want to be delayed by even a few seconds for someone who has to stop by the doors because they only need twenty more steps and don't want to overdo it. I get it. I unbuckle and get out.

When Mom comes around to get into the driver's seat, I pull her into my arms and say, "I love you."

A Dish Served Lukewarm

NATURALLY YOU'RE WONDERING about Zach. He's not hugely tall but at least when he looks at me he isn't seeing the underside of my nose, which would mean he could look right up my nostrils. That's something I never want anyone to do. Why? Well, for one thing, what if there are boogers? But more important: what if you can see a person's brain by looking up their nostrils and it's colour-coded like the red-green-yellow of curry sauce and like curry, red is the hottest or smartest? What does it mean if you can't see anything at all?

Of course I know everyone has a brain. I haven't been able to have a good look up my nostrils no matter what sort of mirror arrangement I come up with so I can't confirm what colour mine is. Given the things I suck at I'm pretty certain it's not red, though.

If you're wondering, I first thought about this in response to numerous 'don't you have a brain?' questions or 'you're brainless' comments from Brian Trockle. He was the biggest boy in my Grade Three class and you could find him with a flock of adoring smaller boys around him most of the time.

When we moved to the country and I started at the new school, young Master Trockle already had a well-established fan club. He was a bully, but worse, he was a Math Whiz and a Total Teacher Suck-Up. It was soon obvious I was no threat to dethrone him either as the Arithmetic King or Teacher's Pet of Pheasant Hill Elementary.

The first time he called me brainless was in math period. The teacher liked to send half a dozen of us up to the board at the same time, and would then call out the numbers and instruct us to add, subtract, multiply, divide or whatever. It was a race to see who got the answer the quickest. This was supposed to make us better at math and in some twisted universe maybe it did. If you got the answer first, you could go back to your desk. He'd put a tick mark next to your name on the Top Ten list at the side of the board, and send another victim to take your place. I was always one of the last ones left up there, struggling to work out an answer while the rest of the class watched and tittered.

Trockle started whispering "she doesn't have a brain" and his minions laughed like it was the funniest thing they'd heard in their lives so before long he didn't bother to whisper. With only lukewarm reprimands from teachers, Trockle kept at it. When I complained to Mom, she told me to ignore it. In her opinion, it would stop if I did. Well, I don't know what I expected her to do and anyway. She had her hands full with baby Jemmy.

Once, in Grade Five, I beat him up. Brian, not Jemmy. Instead of winning anyone over or making him stop, all it did was get me in trouble. There was the whole parents-to-talk-to-the-principal debacle. No one was on my side.

After that, instead of pounding Brian Trockle, I wrote stories about him. I don't have them anymore but I remember a couple of titles: Brian Trouble Dies a SLOW Death by QUICK Sand which I might recycle as it still holds promise, and Brian Trouble Killed in Cat Curiosity Accident, also good and adaptable to any number of situations. I figured prominently in my stories and was always surrounded by adoring friends. By the time I was in grade eight, Nicole and Jarrett had moved into our neighbourhood and were my friends. I no longer needed pretend friends.

You might be thinking, well she's older and she should be smarter by now, but seeing someone's colour-coded brain by looking up their nose? She's probably about to go off into some other crazy story.

I'd like to point out it's not really a crazy notion. The Egyptians pulled the brains out of dead people they were making into mummies by putting hooks up their nostrils, so it's not a stretch to suggest a person's brain could be seen by looking up their nose. Otherwise where did the Egyptians get the idea?

Don't worry, I do know if you look up someone's nose, at worst all you'll see is boogers. The colour-coded brain idea is just one of the things I do in my mind. I don't want anyone looking up my nose just the same.

Now that I think about it, I won't disqualify Egyptian Brain Drain as a story idea. What if in the story, the person wasn't really dead yet, just paralyzed? Unable to move or speak, they might be conscious of everything going on around them and still feel pain. Imagine how it would feel to have a hook, like a crochet hook, shoved up your nose! Would the person be saved before any brain tissue was removed? Or when only a little bit was stirred up like a lobotomy so they would have a major personality change (and be a good person after that)? Or when there was complete brain removal but their body stayed alive so they could become a zombie sex slave or maybe a trained assassin?

Anyway. I'm guessing Zach and I are about the same height or maybe he's a little taller. He has brown hair, eyes the colour of Dad's rye with no water added, normal-size ears and no hairy moles on his nose or anywhere else I can see. As you would expect of a rugby player, he's muscular, but not in a big bulging way.

Of course I see him around school. He's almost always with his buddies and of course I'm with the Untouchables, except when we're on our way to classes, which is usually a mad scramble especially if you have computer lab, which is in the tower, and then have four minutes to get to math, which is in the basement at the extreme far end of the building.

You might think the basement is a lousy place for classrooms and if so, High Five to you! In the case of math classrooms, it's extra bad. Don't get the idea the windows are little things up at the top of the wall; they're not, they're full-size, it's just that you're looking out a ground level, through some shrubs and so on. The odd time there is a bird to watch but mostly it's just dirt and shrubs. If people walk by, which doesn't happen often for two reasons: one, it's lawn and most people walk on the sidewalk; and two, when I'm in class so is almost everyone else, but if people do walk by all you see is their legs. If there was more visual stimulation I wouldn't be so prone to slipping into a coma because of the numbers going to that black hole in my brain I mentioned.

Oh, before I forget, I'd like to mention the Broom Hilda Protocol. Now nearly everyone calls her that! I've even heard comments about The Coven. People are saying things like, "Hey, Haggedy! Where'd you park your broom?" and so on. It's amazing. All it took was for a few popular guys to start the ball rolling. Mean? You bet! Do I feel bad? What do you think?

Anyway. Back to Zach. All Zach and I have done when we see each other so far is say hi. He knows where my locker is but he hasn't shown up there again. I don't know where his locker is and I'm for sure not going to go scout it out, although I have asked Jimmy to do reconnaissance. If he finds it, I may just casually swing by like I'm on my way somewhere else. Sometime. I'm in no rush. It's only been one and a half school days after all.

Then on Monday afternoon when we're passing on our way to class, he turns to walk beside me. "Hi, Lisa," he says.

"Hi. How are you?" Gnashing of teeth! Other guys are watching! Why couldn't I think of something cool to say?

"I'm good. I'll be even better if you say you'll hang with me after school. We could go for that coffee, or a Blizzard or something if you'd rather."

"Oh! Oh no! I promised a friend..." I admit it, for a second, I think about cancelling my plans with Bailey. Then I give myself a mental kick in the pants. *Something Special*, remember? "Sorry. I have plans."

"Oh hey, it's cool."

"But maybe tomorrow?" I suggest.

"No, sorry, Tuesdays I have practice. How about Wednesday?"

"Yes! Wednesday works," I say. No matter what happens, I'll make it work.

"Great! Text me so I have your number." He pulls a pen out of a pocket on the side of his backpack, takes my hand, turns it palm up, and writes his phone number on it. He smiles and continues on his way. I stand there gawking after him. Sappy, right? Sappy or not, I love it.

You're probably thinking, oh sure, now she'll forget it's there and wash it off the next time she goes to the bathroom or her hands are all sweaty and she'll smudge it. No! As soon as I'm in chemistry class and before I can accidentally smudge it, I enter it in my phone and text him a smiley face emoji. Even though class hasn't officially started yet, I'm careful not to let Mr. Zuck see me doing it. No use alerting him to the fact I have my phone with me.

ON TUESDAY, ZACH SURPRISES me with a visit to my locker right at the beginning of the lunch hour.

"Hey," he says, "you eat lunch in the lunchroom?"

"Yeah...?"

"Mind if I join you?"

Mind? Is he kidding? "Umm, sure," I tell him. If I sound reluctant it's just that I'm in shock. Here's where Peony would give a feel-good buck.

"Great!" he says, and together we stroll into the lunchroom. I lead him to the table in the far corner where you'll always find Jimmy because he makes a point of getting there early enough to save seats for everyone.

I introduce Zach, and Jimmy manages to remain normal and not blurt out anything stupid, but then he's immune to Zach's sex appeal, or at least I think he is.

The rest of the Untouchables show up and it's easy to see from their bug-eyed giggling they're definitely not immune to Zach's appeal and I think they may be looking at me with new respect. I'm sure other girls in the lunchroom have noticed and are envious. I ain't lying, I'm gloating.

While we eat, Zach complains he's having trouble with physics, so naturally Jimmy and Maureen offer to help. They arrange to meet at study hall when they all have a spare on Friday. I'm pretty sure the other girls wish they were taking physics instead of their Susie Homemaker courses. Except Maureen, who I've mentioned is brainy and definitely on course to be accepted at some major university. She seems unaware of Zach's blatant masculinity, but then, she can often be seen looking at Jimmy like he's the Sun and the Moon which proves there's someone for everybody. Not to bash either of them, but even though Jimmy has grown a lot since last spring he's still wiry and a bit underfed looking. In other words, a total opposite from Zach, physically anyway. Also although I haven't looked up his nose, I'm pretty sure Zach is more a green or yellow like me than a red like Maureen and Jimmy.

After lunch, Zach walks me to my locker and before he dashes off to his own, he leans in so close I can almost feel the body heat radiating off him. I note a tiny cute freckle on his ear and smell his cologne.

"See you tomorrow," he says. His voice is low and husky and so sexy and has this heart-stopping grin and he's so close I get a funny feeling, you know, down there.

ARE YOU WONDERING WHAT happened to Trent?

Oddly enough, Trent just faded away. I haven't seen or heard from him since he walked away from me at the horse show. I texted him after the show when I made that "my beautiful horse" comment but he didn't respond.

I figured he was busy with Nicole. At first it bothered me, but I don't mind so much now that I've realized I was lucky he showed his true colours so early on. What kind of boyfriend would he make? And, well, *Zach*. I've put my Kill Trent story on a back burner but I'll get it done as soon as a really good idea comes to me. If you're thinking the crochet hook up the nose would serve him right, I haven't ruled it out, but there's also the Casper Disaster and Slow Death by Quick Sand to keep in mind.

And then.

Wednesday morning, I'm on my way to the corner where the school bus stops, fantasizing about hanging out after school with Zach, when I see Nicole standing in the rain a little apart from the two kids that are there every morning, waiting for the school bus. This stops me in my tracks for a second. I'm wondering what I should say to her when I get there, when Trent's car pulls up beside me. He rolls the passenger window down and says, "Hey, Lisa! Hop in!"

Should I tell him to take a hike? Not a peep since the horse show and out of the blue, this? But then I see Nicole watching us. I pull the door open. I'm looking right at Nicole and I have to admit, I'm considering sticking my tongue out at her, but realize maybe he's going to stop and pick her up, too. So I just pretend I don't see her, and slide into the passenger seat.

"Hey, Lisa! Buckle up," he says, and pulls away. He gives me a sort of sideways glance as he shifts gears. "You're lookin' good!"

Really? Nothing about what happened after the show or why he's ignored me since? I guess in his book, 'see you later' can mean next month. I'm surprised I didn't snort. Instead I say, "Thanks."

He pulls up to the stop sign not three meters from where Nicole stands, then since there's no cross traffic, turns right and we cruise right on by. As we do, she and I make eye contact. Do I stick out my tongue now? No. I just smile.

The important point I want to make is: Nicole warned me to leave him alone, I did, and now this.

Have you heard the Klingon proverb, revenge is a dish best served cold? Not much time has passed so maybe this dish is only lukewarm, but I enjoy serving it just the same.

Trent chats away all friendly without saying anything about Nicole. He says he's busy, there were mid-terms he had to study for, he got his bike fixed, lots going on and so forth. Like it's so time consuming to respond to a text! But that's as close as he comes to apologizing.

I'm mildly surprised to note I don't really care if he doesn't come up with anything or if the only time I ever see him for the rest of my life is when he's driving by. Feeling this way is liberating!

When we pull up in front of the school, I quickly unbuckle my seatbelt, open the door and say, "Thanks for the ride!"

"Just a sec, Lisa," he says.

I'm halfway out or at least I have one leg out, but I stop and turn to face him.

He asks, "You doing anything this weekend?"

"Umm, yeah, I'm pretty busy. You know, exams coming up. Have to ride my horse. Lots going on. Thanks again!" I jump the rest of the way out and shut the door behind me before he can continue the conversation.

I'm not a hundred percent sure I really meant that whole I don't care thing. You know, there's that swoop of brown hair with the blonde part and those sparkling blue eyes. So I run off before I have a chance to say or do something stupid.

I make it through the morning classes and manage to impress Mr. Zuck with a correct answer when he singles me out. It was something about the solubility experiment and as I mentioned, I like the experiments. Turns out I didn't know everything about solubility and it was pretty interesting, so I paid attention.

At lunch, I'm disappointed there was no Zach waiting at my locker. I'm settled in with the Untouchables in the lunchroom when I see him come in. He has Tony and Nathan with him; when he's gone through the cafeteria queue, he spots me and gives a wave. Then all three of them join us.

Daryl Lyn and Sandy are suddenly so bright-eyed and energized you'd think there was some kind of stimulant in the beef barley soup today. Connie asked about my art project instead of going on about the Joys Of Machine Stippling on the quilt she's working on with her aunt.

After lunch, Zach walks me back to my locker, and as he's leaving, turns back and calls out, "Don't forget our date! See you here at dismissal?"

"See you here!" I call back.

You have no idea how many people stopped to gawk. I'm pretty sure that cloud I mentioned floating on a few days ago is more of a magic carpet now.

I settle into my desk, open my biology textbook to the chapter we're working on and get my notebook out. I look up just as a couple of guys come into the classroom. As they walk past my desk, one makes eye contact and acknowledges me with a lift of his chin. The other smiles and says, "Hey, Lisa."

You might think this is a ridiculously common occurrence and not worth mentioning, but for three things: one, I'm an Untouchable; two, they noticed me; and three, they admitted noticing me. It's so astonishing all I can do in response is smile and nod.

He called me Lisa!

AUTHOR'S NOTES

I HOPE YOU ENJOYED *Call Me Lisa* even if you haven't read *Wembly*, the first book in the series. When I wrote *Wembly* I thought it was the end of Lisa Rogney's story, but as I worked on my next thriller, *The Bear Mountain Secret*, Lisa kept invading my thoughts. *Call Me Lisa* is the result. Now I'm working on *Bear Mountain* again, and Lisa is still bugging me. It seems there's more Lisa to come. I hope she can wait until I finish *The Bear Mountain Secret* this time.

If you go to my website, http://www.gaylesiebert.com and join my mailing list, I promise not to overstuff your inbox but I will let you know about new releases.

If you have a few minutes, a review on Amazon or Goodreads would be greatly appreciated. Here is the Amazon link:

getbook.at/callmelisa[1]

Gayle Siebert

January 2019

---

1. http://getbook.at/callmelisa

Don't miss out!

Visit the website below and you can sign up to receive emails whenever Gayle Siebert publishes a new book. There's no charge and no obligation.

https://books2read.com/r/B-A-EAZM-JPAPB

BOOKS 2 READ

Connecting independent readers to independent writers.

www.ingramcontent.com/pod-product-compliance
Lightning Source LLC
Chambersburg PA
CBHW051929160426
43198CB00012B/2081